"There is no succ
's' words sit nearly
sadly, they are ofte
sion of an organization is never more vulnerable than during a transition in leadership. As much as a decade of focus, momentum, and direction can be lost in this season! And the difference between a successful succession and failure—a fumbled process—can mean life or death for the organization. Leaders and boards carry no greater responsibility than to shepherd well this passing of the baton. Peter and Doug have created an invaluable resource to help your ministry bring together 'succession' and 'success.'"

–Dr. Wess Stafford, president emeritus,
Compassion International; author of *Too Small to Ignore:
Why Children Are the Next Big Thing* and *Just a Minute:
In the Heart of a Child, One Moment Can Last Forever*

"Doug and Peter join their expertise with a broad network of succession veterans. This book invites all of us into that network, and we learn valuable lessons in the stories of others."

–Leith Anderson president emeritus,
National Association of Evangelicals;
pastor emeritus, Wooddale Church

"I sure wish I had this when I was transitioning. This book would have been incredibly helpful for me as a leader and for my board during the transition!"

–Dana Doll, program director, Micah 6:8 Foundation;
co-founder, Treetops Collection

"As a professional athlete, we are encouraged to grasp and hold onto that title as long as we can get it. We are disincentivized to pass the baton and invest in our future replacements. But in *Succession*, Peter and Doug do a brilliant job of laying out biblical wisdom for investing in our organizations and successors. Just as Jesus did with his disciples, we are called to joyfully pour into the lives of our successors—shepherding, mentoring, and intentionally working ourselves out of our job."

–Nick Hundley, former MLB catcher of twelve years;
senior director of baseball operations for Major League Baseball

"Doug and Peter have given us an invaluable roadmap that will help the missions of our organizations live on long after we've passed the baton. I love that they've provided mission-driven, practical insights for the outgoing leader, incoming leader, board, and staff."

–Brian Mosley, president, RightNow Media

"This book does a terrific job of describing how we should 'hold loosely' to our leadership positions, always putting the needs of the mission and organization ahead of our own. If the guidance in this book is followed, CEO transition can be life-giving to everyone impacted. Well done, Doug and Peter!"

–David Weekley, chairman, David Weekley Homes

"In my career, I've led at a high level in both Fortune 100 companies and nonprofits. I have personally witnessed many successful successions but an even greater number of failed ones. Having succeeded three tenured CEOs, I highly recommend *Succession* as a tool for any board and executive leadership team navigating the succession planning process."

–Anthony Flynn, chief executive officer,
WorkFaith Connection

"This book should be at the top of every leader's reading list!"

–Dr. Andy Bunn, chief operating officer,
Woman to Woman Pregnancy Resource Center

"Peter and Doug team up to bring organizational leaders a 360-view of what's required to execute an intentional and honoring succession plan. Divided into seven core practices, you'll learn from the stories of those who did it well and others who struggled along the way. The practical action steps after each section bring clarity, provide all the right questions, and prompt deep personal reflection. *Succession* is highly relevant for all CEOs, board directors, incoming leaders, and staff. If that's you, then this is one book you must read!"

–Tami Heim, president & CEO,
Christian Leadership Alliance

"Throughout my career, I've served on many nonprofit boards and witnessed several unhealthy successions. This book is a critical resource for boards and leaders to effectively prepare for a leadership transition. The seven practices outlined in *Succession* are valuable for both nonprofits and businesses, whether public or private. I highly recommend that all CEOs and board members read this book."

–Terry Looper, president and CEO, Texon LP

"'The heart of a successful succession begins with a commitment that the mission matters most.' Peter and Doug lay out the heart and practicalities of a gospel-centered succession that ensures the work of the gospel continues after the current leader transitions. This book will be instrumental for leaders and organizations that want to ensure health for all those involved with a transition. Personally, this has given me insight as we evaluate our next steps of stewarding the organizational visions God has entrusted to us."

–Dr. Benjamin P. Thomas,
co-founder and CEO, B2THEWORLD

"Succession is the inevitable destination for all leaders, and Peter and Doug have written an excellent book on how to navigate these choppy waters. *Succession* focuses first on the heart of the leader before moving to hands-on, practical steps that act as buoys in navigating this process with wisdom and clarity. This is a must-read for every organizational leader that will one day face succession—that is, all of us."

–David Wills, president emeritus,
National Christian Foundation

SUCCESSION

Seven practices to navigate mission-critical
LEADERSHIP TRANSITIONS

PETER GREER &
DOUG FAGERSTROM
with BRIANNA LAPP

Foreword by Dan Busby

Publication, distribution, and fulfillment services provided by Amazon Kindle Direct Publishing. kdp.amazon.com/en_US.

This book may be purchased in bulk for educational, business, or promotional use. For more information, please visit peterkgreer.com.

Cover design by Andrea Fahnestock.

Peter Greer's photo by Michael Rothermel.

Doug Fagerstrom's photo by John Pottinger.

DEDICATION

Throughout my career, God transitioned my missional role and place of service six times. Each transition became another marvelous experience to grow in my profession, turn strangers into friends, and serve others beyond what I could have dreamed. I could dedicate this book to the scores of godly men and women who were with me at various commissioning ceremonies. The list is as meaningful as it is long. At first glance, it seems nearly impossible to choose one person—or even two or three—from this list of influencers. But in reality, my choice is quite simple: There is one person who has journeyed with me through all six transitions. She has been a voice of wisdom in every conversation and a partner in prayer in every succession. She saw what I did not see and said what I needed to hear. We have walked in step throughout this journey, as we left behind certain places and entered into new ones. I dedicate this book to my wife, Donna, my missional partner and the love of my life. –Doug

To HOPE's remarkable relay-race team, specifically Chris Horst and Jesse Casler. Thank you for helping to carry the baton so capably. And to Laurel, the one who runs with me. –Peter

Books by Peter Greer

Mission Drift
(coauthored by Chris Horst)

Rooting for Rivals
(coauthored by Chris Horst)

The Board and the CEO
(coauthored by David Weekley)

The Giver and the Gift
(coauthored by David Weekley)

Created to Flourish
(coauthored by Phil Smith)

40/40 Vision
(coauthored by Greg Lafferty)

The Spiritual Danger of Doing Good
(coauthored by Anna Haggard)

Entrepreneurship for Human Flourishing
(coauthored by Chris Horst)

Mommy's Heart Went POP!
(coauthored by Christina Kyllonen)

Watching Seeds Grow
(coauthored by Keith Greer)

The Redemptive Nonprofit
(coauthored by Praxis)

Books by Doug Fagerstrom

The Ministry Staff Member

The Volunteer

Single Adult Ministry Handbook

Single to Single

The Lonely Pew
(coauthored by James W. Carlson)

Single to God

CONTENTS

Introduction	19
Part 1: Postures	31
1: The Mission: What matters most?	33
2: The Myths: What lies do I believe?	41
3: The Moment: Is it time?	57
4: The Mirror: Where is my identity?	72
Part 2: Practices	88
5: Focus on the Whole Race	91
6: Start Training Now	99
7: Create the Plan	118
8: Listen to the Coach	127
9: Communicate Clearly	134
10: Prepare for the Handoff	144
11: Cheer on the Team	159
Conclusion	166
Acknowledgements	176
Appendices	179

Appendix 1: How prepared are you for   180
your succession?

Appendix 2: Sample survey of staff needs   186

Appendix 3: Hiring a search firm   188

Appendix 4: Suggested timeline for   194
a succession plan

Appendix 5: Unique successions   199

Appendix 6: Annotated bibliography   202

Appendix 7: Audit of current talent and culture   208

Appendix 8: Five mistakes a board should avoid   209

About the Authors   212

About the Organization   214

Related Works   215

Notes   217

FOREWORD

Every leader is an interim leader.

As I write this, it has been just ten days since I stepped down from the role as president of the Evangelical Council for Financial Accountability (ECFA). It has been humbling to serve as president for the last twelve years and to see a growing number of churches, ministries, and leaders around the world step up to embrace accountability. The mission of the ECFA is important to me, and my role has been life-giving.

And it's for this reason, perhaps, that stepping down was, at the same time, one of the most joyous and most challenging parts of my career. While I am thrilled to support our next president and see the ECFA expand its impact on the community, acknowledging my role as an interim leader has been neither easy nor comfortable. And, I have a feeling I'm not alone in that.

Most leaders don't like to think about leaving.

For leaders in faith-based organizations, especially, the thought of transitioning out of our role feels uncomfortable—even risky.

Even though every one of us will transition, few leaders and board members take the time to actively prepare for that day. Too often, this critical moment is met with little forethought, leading to haphazard, last-minute plans that can be devastating to an entire organization.

But successions are one of the most important events in our lives and in the lives of the organizations we lead. If we care deeply about the mission of our organization, we will care deeply about what will happen when we're no longer there. Perhaps one of the healthiest things we could do as leaders is to work to ensure that the mission will extend beyond our own tenure. For followers of Christ, especially, the way we approach a succession is a witness to the world around us.

In his book, *Stewards of a Sacred Trust*, David L. McKenna writes: "Like the ripple effect of a stone tossed into a pond, the top leader's influence will move in waves through generations. No decision of the board, absolutely no decision, is more profound."[i]

Here's the bad news: Succession is difficult, and unfortunately, we don't get much practice to do it well. As many leaders can now attest, inadequate preparation can stymie organizational growth and cause significant damage to the mission.

But, thankfully, there is good news: Successful succession is possible! When it's done well, it can propel an organization to even greater heights. In the pages to follow, you'll read stories of leaders who have successfully passed the baton, improving the organization's effectiveness and strengthening the mission. And, you won't just read their stories; you'll learn the postures and practices that pushed them toward their success.

In *Succession*, Doug and Peter start by examining the heart postures of a healthy transition: debunking succession myths and identifying key attributes, like humility and courage, that equip leaders to look beyond their own tenure. After helping leaders to get their hearts in the right place, they dive into seven practices that empower boards, leaders, and staff to flourish throughout a leadership transition.

While this is primarily a book about succession planning, I'm convinced you will find many other gems—like building strong mentoring relationships and cultivating a culture of honor—that strengthen the entire span of a leader's service and enrich the whole organization.

This book is an invaluable resource for both board members and organizational leaders, and I wish I had it when I was transitioning! By embracing the wisdom in these pages, I believe boards will be better equipped to find new leaders, current leaders will be better prepared to transition, and new leaders will be able to step more confidently into their role, empowering entire organizations to thrive.

Dan Busby

President Emeritus of the Evangelical Council for Financial Accountability (ECFA)

INTRODUCTION

A hush fell over the stadium as teams lined up on the starting line for the 4x100 meter qualifying race for the 2008 Summer Olympic Games in Beijing, China.

With fifteen wins under their belt, the United States was predicted to advance and once again medal in the race. The starting gun went off and the crowd erupted in wild cheers as the world's best raced around the course.

In the final leg of the course, the U.S. was poised to edge out Trinidad and Tobago and seize the win. But in the third and final baton pass, disaster struck. David Patton couldn't get the baton into the hands of his teammate, Tyson Gay. In an unexpected turn of events, the baton fell to the ground and the team failed to finish.

After the race, visibly in shock and disbelief, Tyson shared that he'd "never dropped a stick in [his] life." ESPN harshly summarized that the men's team "gagged at a particularly inopportune time."[i]

An hour and a half later, it was the women's team's turn. Unimaginably, in the final handoff of their 4x100 race, Torri Edwards and Lauryn Williams also dropped the baton after a collision with another runner on the course.

In describing the dropped baton, Lauryn explained, "What I'm telling people is that the stick had a mind of its own. It's not my fault, it's not her fault, it's not either of our fault."[ii]

These botched handoffs prevented the United States from receiving medals in both the men's and women's 4x100 relays. It came down to an inability to pass the baton at the moment that mattered most.

We may not be runners competing for gold, but if we are in a leadership position, there will be a moment when it's our turn to pass the baton. No matter how hard or how long we've been running, there will be a time when it will be someone else's turn to grab the leadership baton and run the next leg.

Our collective experience is that far too often, this critical moment in an organization's history is marked by inadequate preparation, muddied vision, and organizational chaos. Just 17% of organizations have a documented succession plan, which seems ironic given that 100% of leaders will eventually transition.[iii]

Jack Crowley, president of Water Street Mission summarized, "It's remarkable to see the high percentage of transitions that go poorly."[iv] In other words, when it comes to succession, there are too many dropped batons.

How can we make sure we don't drop the baton at our moment of succession?

On Leaving Well

The mission of an organization matters too much to leave the task of succession to haphazard planning. It matters too much to simply hope that everything goes well. Organizational leadership and staff development are far too critical to just "wing it."

In this time of transition, leaders and board members have a central role to play. Their decisions will impact the people around them and the organization where they serve. A successful succession is about preserving the long-term health and vitality of the mission. It's about excitement and anticipation as a new season begins. It's about being prepared, not panicked.

No matter how successful a CEO has been, they are ultimately unsuccessful if they don't help the organization navigate the season of succession. No matter how many goals the executive director has achieved, they will fade into insignificance if they don't achieve the goal of actively preparing for what happens after their departure. No matter how much good they do in their leadership roles, it's not good enough if they don't successfully pass the baton.

Fred Smith, founder of The Gathering, summarized, "How you leave is what people remember the most—even more than what you did while you were there."[v]

As you prepare for this moment, look around. There are outstanding staff members who have served alongside you, wise board members who have protected the mission, and gracious supporters who have partnered with you throughout your leadership journey. Many of them will be impacted by the choices you make during your transition. Transitioning well is an act of love and service to those around you and to those whom your organization serves.

With planning and preparation, we believe it is possible for leadership transition to be marked by gratitude and celebration, not anxiety and concern. This moment can be one where the board and staff have confidence in the incoming leader and in the direction of the organization.

On succession planning, Greg Barnes, vice chairman and president of Faith Search Partners nonprofit search division, states it well: "Succession planning is one of the most important acts of stewardship an organization must undertake."[vi]

Yet, many CEOs, executive directors, boards, and leadership teams lack a blueprint for how to transition well. Sound familiar? Then, this book is for you. We hope this book empowers you to do the mission-critical work of navigating a leadership transition, ensuring a firm baton pass in the race that you're running.

Your legacy will be defined and your organization shaped by the decisions and actions during this critical moment.

Dropped Batons

Fifteen years ago, Marc[vii] noticed a significant need for financial services among vulnerable families in his community. With a background in personal finance, Marc founded a nonprofit to provide affordable financial counseling services.

Marc believed in his mission and pinpointed a clear need in the community. With the help of his charismatic personality, the nonprofit grew steadily with consistent funding from donors and corporate partners. Just a few years after the organization's founding, however, the market started to shift—and

Marc rebranded his organization to keep in line with current trends and community needs. They successfully pivoted and entered into a new season of growth.

The team expanded, new donors came on board, and the impact continued. On the surface, this was the story of a thriving nonprofit.

As he navigated the growth and new direction, Marc started to realize he didn't have the right skills or experience to lead the organization in this new season. Instead of stepping down or delegating responsibility to others, he focused on what he knew and tried to secure more contracts for the nonprofit's services. But with low quality control and rapid growth, the organization started to crumble. Money became tight, making it difficult to invest in a chief financial officer or development director. Without the board's careful attention, the financial reserves drained quickly.

Burned out and burdened with the organization's financial insecurity, Marc gave the board a few weeks' notice and left. His sudden exit sent shockwaves through the organization; it was the beginning of the end.

After his departure, the nonprofit endured five more leadership transitions, each lasting less than a year. Just four years after Marc resigned, the organization dissolved.

The baton was never passed, the next runner was not prepared, and the board was unable to coach the organization through this critical transition.

Marc's story is not an isolated case.

Stumbling

Throughout our careers, we've had firsthand experience with organizations that have faltered in this pivotal moment. We have spent our careers in education, global economic development, marketplace ministry, and church. We have seen how critical this moment is for an organization. While we have seen transitions succeed, we've seen far too many successions falter, resulting in a disproportionate amount of hurt and confusion.

In the past year alone, we've had direct experience with several prominent organizations who have stumbled through significant leadership transitions, despite what seemed like a thoughtful, prayerful, and detailed process.

In some cases, there is the sudden awkwardness of a mailed letter describing how the leader "needs to spend more time with family." Few believe the accuracy of this letter, which is only exacerbated by its out-of-the-blue nature. Questions arise about what must have really happened.

Or the leader transitions and the new appointment lasts less than a year. The brevity of the second transition makes it inescapably clear that something went very wrong in the selection process.

Or the leader never really transitions and casts a shadow that undermines the next leadership team. Everyone feels the need for breathing room, but the previous leader is unable to truly walk away.

Or the leader transitions suddenly without a plan in place. The board scrambles to find a solution, but there is a prolonged period of marked instability.

Or a colleague or board member makes a bold move that resembles an attempted coup d'etat instead of a healthy transition of leadership.

Or a donor or board member begins the lobbying process with a strong argument for a son or daughter to be the heir apparent, sabotaging the recruitment process.

Or the process is marked by good intentions and diligent execution, but voices of dissent stall forward momentum and undermine the new leader.

These are not hypothetical scenarios. We have seen these with real organizations, and our guess is that you have, too.

Instead of sitting in judgement about the transitions that ended poorly, our thoughts turn inward:

How do we ensure this kind of story doesn't become our story? How can we work now to ensure a successful succession later?

Neither of us took a course in college or graduate school on succession planning. If it was mentioned during a course in organizational behavior, very little was said. At the time, we were probably far more interested in landing a job than thinking about eventually moving on from it. We were also not taught to think critically about succession.

Compounding the difficulty of navigating a succession well is that we typically don't get a lot of practice doing it. Unlike athletic training, an organization isn't able to run through the plays in practice to get it right before the game. It's not like monthly financial closes or the annual review processes that are built into the normal rhythms of an organization. For the healthiest organizations, leadership transitions are infrequent. Perhaps it's no surprise that few transitions go as hoped.

Methodology, Audience, and Framework

There are many helpful books and articles about succession planning, some of which we have included in Appendix 6. Our hope is that this book would be a concise, biblically grounded, actionable resource to help leaders and boards navigate this moment of transition with excellence. It is filled with real stories of success and failure to help you find the best path forward in advancing the mission.

Perhaps it's not surprising that a book written by two nonprofit leaders is primarily geared toward a nonprofit audience. While we recognize that the specifics of succession in the for-profit and nonprofit sector can look different, many of the core issues and practices are the same. Whatever missional business you are in, we hope there are practical takeaways that assist you in your leadership development and succession planning.

While much of this book speaks specifically to the outgoing leader, we intentionally include points of application for the board, incoming leader, and staff. For a healthy transition, all stakeholders need to be engaged and involved.

In our research for this book, we interviewed dozens of leaders from a variety of sectors who experienced a succession. Whenever possible, we sought out the leader who entered as well as the one who exited. We are grateful for the candid way these leaders shared their successes, but even more significantly, their regrets, failures, and lessons learned. Their courage has allowed us to learn from their wins and learn even more from their missteps. In limited cases, we have changed names and details to protect the identity of the person and organization.

Early in our discussions with leaders who have navigated moments of transition, we realized that successful successions require much more than a mere checklist of best practices. In fact, succession starts by preparing hearts and attitudes and then focuses on the right process and practices.

Phil Clemens, a marketplace leader who currently serves on over a dozen boards summarized, "For faith-based nonprofits, succession planning is especially difficult. Why? Because you're doing God's work. Often, we believe that God wants us to continue the work that He has called us to do. When faith-based nonprofit leaders go through a succession process, it might feel like quitting or giving up."[viii]

But we know this is simply untrue. Jesus Himself spent three years training and equipping a group of twelve disciples, while recognizing that He was going to leave them. In fact, He spent his final day before his arrest pouring into the twelve disciples, who would be integral to the next chapter of ministry and the global expansion of faith.

Just because Jesus returned to Heaven didn't mean He didn't complete God's mission for His life.

Quite the opposite! As He fulfilled His mission, He empowered His successors to carry the Gospel message even further. He said they would do "even greater things."[ix]

The first section of this book focuses on the heart postures that are prerequisites for a healthy succession, and the second section outlines specific practices. In the final pages, we've included appendices with practical tools and checklists that we've found to be helpful. We hope these materials assist you in the preparation and implementation of your organizational succession plan, as they have in our own.

When family or friends hear us talking about this book, they inevitably ask, "When are you transitioning?" Candidly, we don't know the answer to that question! But we do believe that it's a day sooner than it was yesterday, and because we care so much about the organizations we lead, we want to be prepared. We want you to be prepared, too. We are all in the midst of our own succession, and our exit is the final step.

Our hope and prayer is that you would have the courage to do the difficult work of preparing for the day when you transition. May we all lead and leave in a way that we hear "well done, good and faithful servant."

Part 1:

POSTURES

Pick up any book on for-profit succession, and you'll find that a significant percentage of the content addresses the financial requirements to transition a business: ownership, stock, valuation, tax implications, banks, estate plan, liquidity, dividend policy, and more. But for nonprofits and missional businesses, the primary consideration isn't ownership. Rather, we have the tremendously high calling to steward the mission.

In this first section, we explore the postures that help leaders to prepare their hearts for transition. The first four chapters examine the following:

1. The Mission: What matters most?
2. The Myths: What lies do I believe?
3. The Moment: Is it time?
4. The Mirror: Where is my identity?

Before we dive into the practices of successful succession, we must ensure our hearts are in the right place.

1

THE MISSION: WHAT MATTERS MOST?

"The graveyards are full of indispensable men."

–Charles de Gaulle

In Japan, there is a hotel called Nishiyama Onsen Keiunkan that is built around healing hot springs. This hotel has been operating continuously since 705 A.D., making it the longest continuously running hotel in the world. Even more impressive is that this hotel has been run by the same family for fifty-two generations. They have discovered a way to protect the mission, pass on leadership, and see their tenure as only a small part of a much longer and more significant history.

In reading reviews of the hotel, we learn that staff excel in caring for their guests. This flows from a collective belief that each team member is deeply committed to protecting the mission and reputation of the establishment. As one report summarized, they "put their all into offering a spirit of service that stems from a shared desire to protect the inn. This unflagging commitment and hospitality is drawing attention from the hotel industries worldwide."[i]

Their team is focused on the mission, understanding their individual roles as part of a larger story.

Each of us is part of a mission that extends beyond the brief moment that we are entrusted to steward it. Preparing for succession begins with an invitation to look far beyond the confines of our office, our strategic objectives, and our tenure.

The heart of a successful succession begins with an understanding that the mission matters most.[ii] Our leadership is about stewardship for a limited season of time.

Number our Days

While this might be slightly macabre, in my (Peter's) desk drawer, I keep two letters: my resignation letter and my eulogy. My resignation letter reminds me that one day I will leave my role, and my eulogy reminds me to live today in light of what matters most.

While there are so many uncertainties in life, there is no uncertainty about whether we will transition from our role and whether we will one day breathe our last. When asked what surprised him most about life, Billy Graham answered simply, "The brevity of it."[iii]

As Moses writes in Psalm 90, "Teach us to number our days, that we may gain a heart of wisdom." When we carry God's perspective of our life, our perspective moves from nearsighted and temporal to global and eternal.

How would our leadership be different if we lived every day in light of the fact that we will eventually pass it on? How would it change if we became more aware of our mortality? In an attempt to explore this, I decided to write my eulogy. When I first told my wife, Laurel, about the idea, she laughed and said I was crazy. When I told her I wanted to invite my family and friends to my 40th birthday party and read it to them, she was certain I'd lost it.

Perhaps unsurprisingly, my eulogy had nothing to do with the kinds of things I have on my resume, nothing about my jobs or titles. It had everything to do with people, with issues of faith and love, and with gratitude to God and others. And after reading it to my family, we ate carrot cake, because carrots make it healthy, right?

And then we went on imperfectly loving each other.

That exercise allowed me to see the stark contrast between eulogy virtues and resume virtues, as author David Brooks writes about so brilliantly in his book *The Road to Character*. It's far too easy to spend our best energies building resumes and our last days regretting it. In the end, none of our accomplishments, titles, or roles matter nearly as much as we think they do. When we stand before God, will the successes of even the biggest world-changer look anything but petty?[iv]

Beyond my eulogy, I wrote my resignation letter as a similar exercise to remember that one day I will walk out of my place of work. My days in my current role are numbered. One day, that letter will be opened by the board of directors. Hopefully, that day will also be marked by carrot cake and a celebration of all that God has done throughout this season.

This last day of work in our current role is coming for each of us.

Remembering our mortality helps us live today with purpose and clarity about what matters most. Similarly, remembering that we will one day transition from our current role invites us to build an organization to outlast any one season of leadership. We are entrusted with leadership for a limited time and the final question will be how well we hand the baton to our successor to carry on the mission.

Focus on the Cathedral

Our vocations are callings from God, based on our gifts, passions, experiences, and opportunities. Our work is purposeful, and it is part of something so much bigger than merely our season of service.

Have you heard the old tale of the construction crew queried by a passerby?

"What are you doing?" a passerby asked the first worker.

"Stacking bricks," he said flatly.

"And how about you?" a second worker was asked. "What are you doing?"

"Mixing cement," he grunted.

Looking to the third worker, the passerby inquired, "And what are you doing?"

"I'm building a cathedral!" came the enthusiastic reply.

It's easy to get ground down by the day-to-day tasks of mixing cement and stacking bricks. In the Middle Ages, thousands of "working stiffs" devoted their whole lives to doing that very thing, erecting places of worship that they would never see completed in their lifetime.[v] This was the story of Abraham and Sarah, Moses, John the Baptist, and many other biblical heroes. Their mission grew and expanded long after they had passed. At the end of Hebrews 11, the writer notes that the many heroes of the faith were "commended for their faith, yet none of them received what had been promised, since God had planned something better for us so that only together with us they would be made perfect."[vi]

What would it look like for us to carry this perspective into the organizations where we work and the missions we work toward?

We can follow in the footsteps of saints throughout history who worked with devout hearts and eyes of faith—people who are now receiving their eternal reward. While we have yet to see the fulfillment of our work, Paul offers a word of encouragement: "Whatever you do, work at it with all your heart, as working for the Lord, not for human masters, since you know that you will receive an inheritance from the Lord as a reward. It is the Lord Christ you are serving."[vii] Our lives are merely a drop in the ocean in view of eternity, and the missions of the organizations we lead are simply a gift to temporarily steward in the limited time we have been given.

"If our missions don't span generations, they're probably limited to human ambition," shares Justin Straight, co-founder of LoanWell.[viii] As we think about succession planning, let's begin with a fierce commitment to the mission that far outlasts any one leader's tenure.

Jesus reminds us to "not store up for yourselves treasures on Earth."[ix] Just as death has a way of reminding us to make the most of life, an eye on succession has a way of reminding us to make the most of the opportunity to lead our organizations now.

How would we lead differently if we lived every day in light of our inevitable succession?

ACTION STEPS:

The Mission: What matters most?

1. **Outgoing Leader:** Are there ways that your

leadership is focused on your own legacy instead of a bigger Kingdom vision? Consider writing your resignation letter as a way to help you remember that there will come a day when you transition. Articulate your vision for the organization that you hope extends far beyond your tenure.

2. **Incoming Leader:** Take time to surrender your calling to God, asking for guidance, wisdom, and a humble heart as you walk through the next steps in the transition process.

3. **Board:** As guardians of the mission, have you done the difficult work of staying true to the organization's mission? Is there anything more that you can do to ensure leadership understands the difference between laying bricks and building a cathedral? Regularly evaluate if the mission is too closely intertwined with one leader.

4. **Staff:** Take time to reflect: What were the things that initially drew you to the organization? What excites you most about the mission? (It's common to have questions when a leader mentions his or her transition, but starting the conversation does not mean imminent transition.)

2

THE MYTHS: WHAT LIES DO I BELIEVE?

"Nothing is more difficult than competing with a myth."

–Francoise Giroud

Jena Lee Nardella founded Blood:Water with the band Jars of Clay when she was just 21 years old. Since 2004, the organization has supported grassroots organizations fighting the HIV/AIDS and water crises in sub-Saharan Africa. Garnering national attention,

Jena mobilized resources, built a global team, and spoke around the country.

After years with Blood:Water, Jena started to think about her own transition and the nonprofit's succession plan. Unsure if she was the one to lead the organization through its next season of growth, Jena started to verbally process her own uncertainty to her board, and the board went into panic mode. She shared, "I didn't have the courage or the awareness to recognize that that was probably the point when I should've been doing my own work in transitioning and then come very clearly and boldly to the board with a plan and timeline."

Out of deep admiration and respect for Jena, the board promised to do whatever Jena needed to keep her in leadership. They backed her with energy and support, hired a managing director to take over operational details, and gave Jena a sabbatical.

And while their unwavering support was very generous, Jena admits that it didn't fix the underlying issue. She was relieved from many of her responsibilities and had a wonderful sabbatical with her family, but she still came back to the organization with all of the same inner challenges.

"Because I was afraid and because my whole identity was wrapped up in Blood:Water, I felt like everyone was counting on me. Even though I wasn't sure if I should be the leader for the next stage of the organization, I didn't feel like I had permission to question it."

The board did its best to try to keep Jena within the organization while relieving her of some key executive pressures. This resulted in significant restructuring within the organization, which promoted a new CEO from within the executive team and repositioned Jena as chief strategy officer. At the same time, Jena remained on the board as a non-voting member: still a force within the organization without the authority. This gave the board a sense of continued confidence that the organization would stay on track since Jena was still around.

But things were not on track.

As one could imagine, the restructuring created role confusion across the team, programs, and donors. The organization began to move in an unhealthy direction, but it was overlooked by the board due to the lack of clear communication, poor accountability structures, and an underlying assumption that everything was alright because Jena was still around.

The new chief executive left and growth stalled. Because there was a gap, the board asked Jena to take on the interim director position. She worked remotely as the interim director for six months as the organization continued to undergo hefty restructuring and change. The sudden change in leadership caused significant strain not only for her personally but for the ministry as well. "I had no idea finding a replacement was going to be so difficult," she shared.

It's been six years since that time, and Blood:Water is still managing the impact of a difficult transition. "We have a redemption story and gobs of grace," Jena shares, acknowledging the strong leadership team in place and the organization's health now. "But it took six years."[i]

Looking back, Jena sees many ways that she would have handled her transition differently. She wishes that she had mustered the courage to say to herself that it was time to change. She wishes she had taken the time to process her transition on her own before telling her board or staff. And while grateful for her board's support, she wishes the board had put the health of the organization first.[ii]

Kim Jonker and William F. Meehan III write that transitions become especially difficult "when board members' respect for that [leader] compromises their ability to act with resolve. Long friendships can be put at risk, tight-knit boards can unravel, and organizations can lose their focus—all because a board is unwilling or unable to ensure a strong transition to the next generation of leadership."[iii] To honor the leader and the mission requires the board to have an honest conversation about succession planning.

Today, Jena is using her experience to provide coaching, mentoring, and guidance to dozens of nonprofit leaders each year through Praxis and their nonprofit accelerator program. Many nonprofit leaders have made their own transitions of leadership with far less turbulence than she experienced as a result of her wisdom and guidance.[iv]

Embedded in any discussion of succession are several insidious myths that can undermine a healthy transition. Most often, they are not stated explicitly, yet they lurk in boardrooms and in the recesses of our hearts. The groundwork of healthy succession planning begins by naming some of the most prevalent myths that sabotage healthy transitions.

Myth 1: I'm indispensable.

During a pick-up game of soccer with friends, I (Peter) collided with a teammate on the field. The collision didn't just shatter my ankle—it shattered the myth of my own importance. It was the moment when I realized my own replaceability, and it was the most freeing moment of my career.

As paramedics hastily carried me off of the field on a stretcher, my mind raced frantically. It seemed like my accident couldn't have come at a worse time. Early the next morning, I was scheduled to be on a plane to Dallas, then Houston, then Raleigh. A few days later, I was slated to deliver a talk in Santa Barbara and then Orange County. With my ankle precariously bent at an angle that the human ankle was never designed to bend, it was instantaneously clear that I was going to miss our largest fundraising events of the year.

"Will we have to cancel the events?" I wondered.

Before I had even been discharged from the hospital or had time to wrestle through these questions, my colleagues began responding with thoughtful action. Within a matter of hours, my flights had been canceled and plans had been set in motion for team members to step in and take my place at each event. With grace and incredible speed, these friends deftly covered all of my responsibilities.

As the following weeks of events unfolded, I kept my ankle elevated on the couch and wondered what would happen to our budget. Would my absence negatively impact our fundraising targets?

The results were not as I expected. Without exception, the funds raised at each event exceeded previous years' generosity. Both HOPE International and the rest of the world kept on spinning.

After one event, I received a text that read, "Of course you were missed by those of us who have a personal love for you and your family, but it was evident this morning that others can equally do the job." In other words, "We missed you. But everything went beautifully without you."

Listening to the response from those in attendance at each event, it's clear that my colleagues didn't simply do the job; they knocked it out of the park.

This injury turned into one of the most liberating moments of my career. Our mission will undoubtedly carry on with excellence when the time comes for my transition.

In fact, I'm convinced that one of the highest compliments a leader could receive in the midst of a transition is if everyone—staff, outgoing leader, incoming leader, management, board, and clients—thought, "We'll miss you, but your absence won't be such a big deal."

We like to be needed, and the idea that we are somehow indispensable to the mission feels good. Far too often, our first thoughts are focused on us and our tenure instead of the mission and future of the organization. We can be people with giant egos and myopic vision. Yet, concern for organizational health requires that we place the mission above our egos and refuse to sabotage or limit long-term organizational impact.

Marty Ozinga III—CEO of a fourth-generation family business to provide concrete, bulk materials, and energy solutions to communities—shares, "We're not working here for ourselves; everything belongs to God. If you take the ego out of the picture, if you're not working for yourself (and asking 'what do I get out of it?') and rather ask, 'how do I serve others?' ... that's the secret to success.'"[v]

Leaders who successfully transition understand that they are not indispensable. They refuse to build a fragile organization precariously balanced on their own egos or the need to feel significant. They see other internal leaders as capable and invest in their development. Desiring to share their platform and ensure the organization is not reliant on any one person, they seek to give away authority and decision-making power. They treat their colleagues with the highest respect, knowing that a colleague may be in their role one day. There is a joy in letting go and watching others take over important operational decisions.

When John Coors Sr. was facing retirement

from CoorsTek, Inc.—a fifth-generation, family-owned global manufacturer of engineered ceramics—his three sons appointed his namesake, Jonathan, with the arduous task of asking dad if it was time to step down. With every ounce of fear and nervous energy, younger Jonathan met his dad at their favorite coffee shop to have the conversation. He barely got the words of transition out of his mouth when his dad quickly responded, "How about tomorrow?!" John Sr. was ready to let go and excitedly watch the next generation step up to lead.[vi]

When we step down, someone else will step up. When we let go, we let God be God.

It might be a tough conversation with a trusted son or an accident worse than a soccer field collision. It might be a calling to somewhere new or the high calling of caring for a family member. Regardless of the reason, the world will keep on spinning and the healthiest organizations will continue flourishing when the moment of departure arrives.

Many times, the health of an organization is predicated on humility in its top leaders. It is crucial that we do not harbor any illusion that we are indispensable. We might be surprised at the timing of transition, but we shouldn't be surprised at the transition itself. That day is coming for each one of us!

We are not indispensable—and that realization is wonderfully freeing.

Myth 2: I'll get around to it.

In a small, semi-rural community, hundreds of teenagers showed up each week to an abandoned schoolhouse. It had been creatively transformed into the church's youth center where two or three of the teens regularly would give their lives to Jesus each week. Youth leader Aaron and his wife, Sophie,[vii] were energized and excited by the ways God was clearly moving and transforming lives.

After three years, God called the couple to move to another state to help revive a struggling ministry. It was a difficult decision to leave behind their students and the ministry they dearly loved. In tears, the couple packed up their family and moved miles away to begin a new chapter of ministry.

They left with gratitude for all that happened in this church and excitement for their next assignment. What they hadn't planned for was what would happen to the ministry after they departed. With no clear succession plan or leaders to step in, the ministry began to falter and quickly lost momentum. Most of the teens stopped gathering at the old schoolhouse.

Today, there are fewer than a dozen teenagers

attending the church. Reflecting back, Aaron notes that it was irresponsible to focus on where he was going with no thoughts or plans about leaving well. It was poor stewardship to avoid planning for what would be left behind.

In some cases, leaders don't take the time to plan for their succession. Other leaders may understand the necessity of succession planning and fully intend to prepare, but they fail to make time for it until it's too late. Both are dangerous to an organization and its mission.

A mission may be vibrant and its impact transformative, but if there is no plan for what will happen after a leadership transition, the impact will likely be timebound and eventually crumble.

Why is actively planning and preparing for a succession so rare? Mark Linsz, co-founder of My Next Season, an organization specifically built to help leaders navigate their transitions, shares the one thing that leaders all have in common: They are busy! They're hardworking people committed to valiant missions.[viii] What effective leader doesn't have more to do than time to do it? Daily, there are operational, financial, and human resource issues to attend to and fires to put out.

Here's the hard truth: If we don't set aside and

protect time for succession planning, it simply won't happen. While everyone may be a fan of succession planning in theory, few prioritize it.

Many of us can fall into the trap of believing that we'll have margin down the road to focus on succession planning. But if we're waiting for margin to suddenly appear, we'll be waiting ... and waiting ... and waiting.

Mario Zandstra serves as the president and CEO of Family Legacy, a ministry to orphaned and vulnerable children in Lusaka, Zambia. As a seasoned leader, Mario has observed, "If you plan a succession well, you might lose your job early. But if you plan too late, you might lose the organization."[ix]

Mission-driven leaders make succession planning an annual conversation, at least. They build structures to ensure that this conversation is not lost among many other competing demands.

Myth 3: No one will do this job as well as me!

When Collin[x] came into his role, his predecessor delivered a three-page letter to the board, outlining all of the reasons why Collin was the wrong person for the role. In essence, the letter described why Collin was an inferior choice to lead the organization and cataloged the ways in which he would inevitably fail. There was no ambiguity in the words that each board member read: the person you hired can't possibly do the job as well as I can! In doing this, the predecessor actively undermined not just Collin's role but the health of the entire organization.

When we care deeply about an organization, it's easy to believe that no one will do the job quite as well as us. No one will care quite as much as we do. No one will give quite as much as we have. Especially for founders, it's difficult to think about someone else carrying on the vision with as much passion and clarity.

Mario Zandstra reminds us, "Pride is the issue that holds the outgoing leader back and the incoming leader from going forward."[xi]

Hubris, fear, and insecurity commonly prevent transitioning leaders from believing that there are others who could not only do the job well, but do it better. Great leaders are not intimidated by the strengths of others; instead, they choose to strengthen the people they hire. One of a leader's most important roles is to build a team and culture that intentionally outlasts them. (For more information on building a lasting team, see chapter 6.)

ACTION STEPS:

The Myths: What lies do I believe?

1. **Outgoing Leader:** Review the myths presented in this chapter. Which is the most significant obstacle for you to overcome in order to
experience a healthy transition of leadership?
Write down any attitudes or obstacles that
might prevent you from letting go. How could
you begin to prepare yourself to leave, even
if you believe your transition is years away?

2. **Incoming Leader:** Consider the myths that
you have paid attention to in your transition.
Ask the Holy Spirit to point out any pride or
fear that may prevent you from leading with excellence in this next season. Guard your heart
and mind through the transition and beyond
it in order to lead with humility and grace.

3. **Board:** Engage the leader in candid conversations about a stewardship versus ownership
mindset. Give time annually to the topic of
transition, so that it's not a surprise when the
moment arrives. Are there myths that the board
has succumbed to when considering transition?

Myth	Key Attribute	Truth	Corrective Pursuits
I'm indispensable.	Pride	The mission matters most.	Invest in the development of colleagues and give away decision-making power.
I'll get around to it.	Busyness	Succession planning starts now.	Set aside time for succession planning and make it an annual conversation with the board.
No one will do this job as well as me.	Insecurity	There are people who will do this job well—and even better.	Build a team and a culture that intentionally outlasts the current leadership.

How can you work together to overcome these myths and lead well in preparing for succession?

4. **Staff:** Which myth sticks out the most to you? Are you guilty of believing any of these myths yourself? Invite the Holy Spirit to break down the myths you might be telling yourself. Find ways to encourage the outgoing or incoming leader in his or her own leadership journey.

3

THE MOMENT: IS IT TIME?

"Time is what we want most but what we use worst."

–William Penn

When Robert Mugabe was elected as executive president of Zimbabwe in 1987, the nation and the world celebrated. In the week he was elected, Mugabe told TIME Magazine, "We are beginning a completely new chapter."[i]

Zimbabwe, in their newfound independence, celebrated Mugabe and the early economic boom in his presidency. But just four months into his leadership, things changed. Mugabe declared that he would transform the country into a one-party Marxist state. An independence initially marked by joy and celebration quickly turned to violence and corruption as Mugabe squashed protests and silenced rivals.

By 2007, Mugabe's rule "yielded 1,700% inflation, an 80% unemployment rate, and average life expectancy of 35, the lowest in the world."[ii] His insatiable hunger for power blinded him to the needs of his people and drove him to cling even more tightly to his presidency.

When he lost the 2008 election, Mugabe demanded a recount and shut down the distribution of international aid within Zimbabwe. His opponent withdrew, and Mugabe refused to relinquish control for almost another decade. "Only God who appointed me … will remove me," he said. He finally resigned under intense pressure from the military and political rivals in 2017, just two years before his death.[iii]

Mugabe just didn't know when it was time to leave, and the country paid a severe price. His unwillingness to step down for the good of his nation plunged Zimbabwe into economic and political turmoil that continues to this day.

We're unlikely to turn into corrupt dictators,

but we can certainly overstay our effectiveness.

While many do not have official term limits, we've all seen leaders who have stayed in their role long past their prime. We don't want to be the type of leader who is the only one in the room unaware that it's time for a transition.

In the healthiest transitions, there is a freedom to let go. Dr. Peter Teague, who recently transitioned from serving as president of Lancaster Bible College, notes, "Leaders who have experienced a long, fulfilling run need to consider sharing the blessing with another person."[iv]

Divine Promptings

Getting the timing of a transition right requires us to be attentive to where God might be leading. If we keep running hard enough and fast enough, we will never be open to the Holy Spirit's prompting that it might be time to transition.

Nathan Sheets, founder of I am Second and Nature Nate's Honey, notes that we ignore God's prompting at our own peril.

In October 2009, Nathan sensed the Lord prompting him to leave I am Second, the organization he had founded less than a year earlier. He shares, "I took this prideful position in my heart: Lord, how could you do I am Second without me?" He admits that he shut down the promptings he sensed from the Holy Spirit and didn't step down.

He didn't anticipate what would happen next.

In the six months that followed, an inappropriate relationship with a colleague forced him to leave I am Second suddenly and in a way that he never would have expected.

As he, his wife, and the ministry reeled (and healed), Nathan repented and sought counseling. The healing process was long and arduous. Unemployed, he prayed and asked the Lord to provide the next direction.

The Holy Spirit started prompting him again, this time to expand his honey hobby into a full-time business. And this time, with humility and conviction, Nathan listened. Today, Nature Nate's Honey can be found on grocery shelves across America—success that Nathan and his wife, Patty, attribute only to God.[v]

Whatever the season, divine promptings are a gift. From the beginning of time, God has guided people with gentle (or not so gentle) nudges, and Scripture records a host of men and women who responded differently to them. For the Israelites, disobedience to God's prompting meant wandering in the wilderness for forty years before reaching the Promised Land.

But for others who obeyed—no matter the risk—joy and trust followed their step of faith. For Esther, it meant risking her life to save the lives of a nation. For Daniel, it meant devoting himself to prayer in the face of a dangerous decree. For Peter, it meant stepping out of the boat at the risk of drowning.

Navigating a succession requires surrender: a willingness to stay and a willingness to go. In his book, *Living in Bonus Time*, Alec Hill writes, "For Christians, the request for direction begins with a bow of the knee. Surrender—freely choosing to place ourselves under God's will—is self-emptying and often difficult. Clearly countercultural to notions of self-assertion and independence, it requires humbling ourselves. Brother Lawrence labeled this 'hearty renunciation.' Thankfully, our submission is not into the hands of a tyrannical abuser but to a loving Father."[vi]

Successful successions require a sensitivity to the Spirit's leading and courage to open our hands to wherever and whenever God leads. It's living with a commitment to following God's leading to anything, anywhere, at any time.

Know the Organization's Season

As Southern New Hampshire Rescue Mission was beginning a new strategic plan period, Rick Rutter, the executive director at the time, sensed that God was telling him that the next stage of the organization wasn't his to lead. He remembers sensing from the Lord, "This isn't for you to do. This is for someone else to do."

And after a year and a half of prayer and intentional conversations with pastors and mentors, Rick stepped down. Having experienced poor transitions in the past, Rick was intentional to create a smooth transition process, so that all stakeholders felt secure and had the space to ask questions. He connected with the board, ensuring that each member had clarity of vision and mission. By recognizing his own giftedness and limitations, Rick was prepared to leave. He even "looked forward" to handing off the baton.

Even after his transition, he was careful not to overstep. His focus on the mission caused him to say, "I am always ready and willing to help, but I will never overstep my bounds or overstay my welcome." He advocated for the mission and provided wise counsel to the new leader, but only when his successor asked for help.[vii]

In each new stage of organizational growth, certain skills are required to drive the mission forward. The skills needed to start a ministry as an entrepreneur, for example, differ from the skills needed to scale an established organization. Similarly, each growth stage of an organization will require different expertise.

Every three years in the executive evaluation, Jack Crowley asks himself and his team to consider the following questions: What kind of organization are we in this season? What type of leader do we need now? Is it still me?[viii]

Regularly asking "What kind of leader does the organization need at this particular moment?" helps us to continue growing and learning, and it protects us from overstaying our effectiveness. Remember, it's always best to leave before everyone is eager for you to go!

Too often, society questions leaders who decide to leave their organization before retirement. Yet, in many cases, these are leaders who are seeking to honor the mission above self-preservation. They are willing to candidly assess when their skills and abilities no longer meet the needs of the organization. They're unafraid to ask if it's time for another person to lead.

Do we trust that God has others who could lead even better than us? Do we trust that God who led us to this role could lead someone else to this role for the next stage of growth and impact? Considering these questions allows us to ultimately ask, "Am I still the right leader for this season?"

It takes courage to ask this question and even more courage to honestly answer it.

Know your Season

It's not enough to look only at the organization's stage of growth when planning for succession; mission-minded leaders are humbly attentive to their own seasons, too.

Helping Up Mission, a nonprofit in Maryland, provides hope and comprehensive restoration programs to men and women who are fighting addiction and homelessness on the streets of Baltimore. Bob Gehman, who serves as the organization's CEO, has led the organization through twenty-one years of growth and three successful capital campaigns. As the team completed the most recent campaign, he led the organization into a new strategic planning process to provide focus and clarity moving forward. And within the strategic plan, he is including a timeline for his own succession. Even in a season of success, Bob is overtly and intentionally preparing the organization for its next steps without him at the helm.[ix]

Similarly, when Arthur Brooks, former president of the American Enterprise Institute, stepped down from his role, many questioned it. After all, he seemed to be thriving in his role. In an interview with POLITICO Magazine, Arthur shared, "The worst possible thing for an organization is when you leave not on top." He continued, "It's counterintuitive. As a steward, as an ethical matter, it's the right thing to do. I have worked my whole career to make this place great. If I leave it when I'm not doing my best work, I've obviated the very ethical point that motivated me to come here in the first place. So I had to practice what I preach."[x]

Leith Anderson shared a story about when he came to the end of thirty-five years of ministry at Wooddale Church in the Minneapolis suburbs. He knew that the transition in this megachurch would be monumental. Shortly after he had developed a succession plan for the board to engage in and follow, he called his mentor, Lyle Schaller, and asked what he should do next. Lyle gave him one word: "Leave." And when the successor was welcomed in, Leith did just that. Since then, Leith has taken on a new role at a different organization. Thanks to Leith's careful succession planning, his wisdom in knowing when to step down, and God's abundant grace, the church has continued to thrive.[xi]

Leaders like Bob, Arthur, and Leith know their season, and they know when it's time to transition.[xii]

By keeping the mission central, they avoid an attitude of entitlement and never use phrases like, "The organization owes me" or "This is my ministry" or "I sacrificed in the beginning, now I deserve some reward." They intentionally make themselves less essential to the mission, and in so doing, are free to avidly pour into and empower others. They cheer on the next leader, hoping that he or she succeeds and helps the organization to reach even greater levels of impact.

In helping leaders to avoid overextending their season, the board has a crucial role to play. Their responsibility is to hold the mission higher than their commitment to the person as a leader. Boards that navigate a succession know that it's possible to overextend grace when we honor the current leader at the expense of the organization.

Is it Time?

What are the signs that it might be time to transition?

It may start with an awareness that your mind isn't as focused on the mission anymore. If your passion for the mission or organization begins to wane, it may be an early indicator that it's time to explore a transition.

Others may begin to feel lingering fatigue and an internal need for change. At times, when leaders have felt this, they've sought a chief operating officer (COO) or sabbatical to alleviate their exhaustion.

There are plenty of times that it is really good (and needed) to take a break. Sabbath is a biblical command. Likewise, there are plenty of times where it is necessary and wise to delegate and hire other senior staff to provide operational support. But this too could be a cover for a more difficult conversation.

It's not wrong to take a sabbatical or hire a COO; we just need to make sure that we're not avoiding a more difficult conversation or an underlying issue. Is it time for a sabbatical, a COO—or is it time to go?

If it's truly time to transition, sabbaticals and COOs won't solve the deeper issue. Are we willing to pause long enough and "get neutral"? As Terry Looper, founder and president of Texon, describes in his book, *Sacred Pace*, getting neutral means setting aside time to pray and seek the Lord until we genuinely want His will more than our own.[xiii]

When Dr. Andy Bunn was preparing his heart for transition, he spent over a month in prayer, both individually and with his wife, asking that the Lord's will and his own would align. "We prayed that the decision would not be one made out of selfish ambition or other misguided thoughts," Andy shared. "I have learned that each role has been a calling and privilege to serve God. I just need to be open to His wisdom and serve Him in whatever capacity."[xiv]

This openness to God's leading is important because the danger is not just that you might leave too late; it's that you might leave too early. This is particularly significant as younger leaders trend toward shorter and shorter tenures with their employers, often at the expense of the organization. Is this a time to depart or to courageously stick with the organization?

As you seek God's direction and evaluate your season, be ready to ask the core questions and honestly answer them.

1. Am I still passionate about the mission of the organization?
2. Am I more nostalgic about the past or energized by where the organization is going?
3. Am I more focused on my own security and status or the needs of staff and stakeholders?
4. Am I constraining the vision or empowering the team to work toward it?
5. Is the organization's identity conjoined with my identity (and vice versa)?
6. Am I still committed to active learning and excellence? Is the organization?
7. How is the organizational culture? Are staff mo-

tivated?

8. Is the board more committed to me as the leader or to the mission? Is there any significant misalignment with the board?

9. Are there difficult conversations that the board or management are avoiding?

10. Am I asking 'What's in it for me?' or 'What's best for the organization?'

11. Are there new opportunities to deepen or enhance the mission that I don't have the interest or energy to take on?

12. Where do I see the organization going in the next 5-10 years? Do I have the skills necessary to lead the organization there?

For the good of the mission and the health of the leader and organization, it's important to courageously ask the difficult questions.

It takes courage and humility for both CEOs and board members to prepare for the moment when a CEO transitions—to ensure that, in a way, his or her absence will not be felt. It takes even greater humility and self-awareness to recognize when it is time for a change. We have an opportunity to point people to Christ in how we handle succession planning.

For all of us, there will be a time when it will be right for us to transition. Let's not overstay our moment. We must pray with our hands and heart open to God's divine leading and with the courage to ask, "Is it time?"

ACTION STEPS:

The Moment: Is it time?

1. **Outgoing Leader:** When it comes to succession planning, what might God be prompting you to do in this moment of your organizational history? Have you paused long enough to listen? If God is prompting you to prepare for your transition, do you have the courage to follow through? Consider going away for a 24-hour retreat at least once a year. As part of that, pray with your hands open for clarity if it might be time to consider a transition.

2. **Incoming Leader:** Open up your hands to be ready to step into the role when it's time. Don't rush it. In the waiting, commit to asking questions—lots of them. Try not to assume anything; rather, learn everything you can about the mission you are now called to lead. Reach out to the board, staff, supporters, and other key stakehold-

ers for all perspectives.

3. **Board:** Without preparation and planning, a leader's transition can blindside organizations, creating turmoil, uncertainty, and a lack of clear direction. Have the board and CEO had the difficult conversations to plan for contingencies in leadership? When was the last time the board had a conversation to assess leadership and discern whether the current leader is the right person to carry the mantle into the next season?

4. **Staff:** How can you be well prepared for the moment that a leader announces his or her transition? Pursue honest dialogue with your direct manager about excitements and fears, questions and concerns. Knowing that everyone will be in a different place of grieving during a transition process, use discernment. Be on guard against unproductive conversations, remaining grounded in hope and joy.

4

THE MIRROR: WHERE IS MY IDENTITY?

"When the incumbent's primary identity is not (or no longer) tied to leading the organization, good succession occurs naturally."

–Price Harding

A decade ago, I (Peter) was navigating the seemingly impossible task of balancing my obligations to my family and my work. We had three kids under age five, coinciding with the most significant operational, financial, and human resource challenges of my career.

Doing an exceptionally poor job keeping my priorities in place, I had been away more than a hundred nights that year. Even on nights that I was physically present at home, my mind was still at work, and I was missing precious family moments. My wife, Laurel, was virtually operating as a single mom. And I was building a "successful" ministry.

I was so focused on the demands and feelings of worth at work that I missed both the joy and significance of my role as a husband and father.

When I finally "came to," facilitated by a very clear and candid conversation with Laurel after the kids were in bed one night, I felt like I was going to have to choose between my work and my family. Being presented with such a stark choice was a gift. It was clear that my family mattered more, and so I began exploring what other organizations, roles, and jobs would allow me to be a better husband and father.

Exploring other positions exposed pride and unhealthy attitudes. Pride in finding too much of my identity in my work. Pride in falsely believing that the organization needed me.

Alongside pride, fear also started to come to light. Fear of how I would be known when no longer serving in my role. Fear of how I would provide for my family. Fear of the uncertainty that comes with transition.

In the end, we navigated that season with new controls in place to help balance work and family priorities. While a job change wasn't needed, a heart change certainly was. Pride and fear are real and dangerous, and they clouded my thinking.

Pride and fear: These two powerful forces work against leaders and undermine healthy successions. When not recognized and addressed in a leader, they can weaken an entire organization and sabotage a succession. These maladies may manifest themselves and rear their unwelcome presence in the CEO's office, the boardroom, and in conversations among staff and constituents.

Before beginning the practices of succession planning, we must undergo heart surgery.

When we can't stop wondering *What will I do next? What if it doesn't work out?*, we start to believe that a career is a freeway with a thousand exits and only one entrance. If we get off to try something new and it doesn't work out, will we ever find our way back?[i]

When we succumb to fear, we spend our time and energy on self-preservation rather than considering long-term organizational health. Fear is an immobilizing enemy, and the questions we must ask ourselves in order to remove its hold are actually quite simple: Can we trust that the God who led us to this ministry cares more deeply about it than we are even capable of caring? Can we trust that God's plan and timetable are perfect? Can we trust that the mission will continue to thrive as God raises up another leader to steward the next season of impact?

While fear looks ahead with anxiety about what's to come, pride looks inward. When it comes to succession planning, pride obsesses over questions focused on us: What will people think of me if the next person succeeds? What will happen to my legacy and systems if the new leader chooses a different direction? Will gaps in my leadership be exposed? Will the next generation know who I am and what I did?

Just thinking about these questions should give us pause. Who is the hero in this story? Are we celebrating our accomplishments or are we celebrating the God who called us to this work and provided everything necessary to accomplish it?

When we allow ourselves to be defined by our

work or a particular role, our identity becomes so enmeshed with a title that giving it up would mean losing part of ourselves.

It's selfishness masked in an illusion of service.

In an organization, this might mean that the leader's name is too closely attached to the organization or that too many conversations begin with "My" or "I." When this is the case, it becomes increasingly easier to lose the missional perspective, replacing the mission with a personality.

After twenty years of leading a thriving ministry, Ed Dobson, a pastor in the midwest, retired after he was diagnosed with ALS. The Sunday evening farewell celebration was second to none. He was loved, honored, and respected for his many years of leadership. But on Monday, no one called. Tuesday was no different. On Wednesday, his cell phone still had not rung. "Why aren't people calling me to ask for my opinion, perspective, or decisions?" he wondered. Convinced his cell phone was out of order, he asked his wife to phone him from their living room. When her call came through, he began to get depressed. It was as if the ministry did not need him anymore. But after thought and prayer, he rejoiced. The ministry was continuing to advance under new leadership. While he knew he was loved, he realized he wasn't needed and the mission was continuing. That was his new joy. That was a reason to celebrate![ii]

Do we know who we are when the phone doesn't ring, when the emails asking for our input on decisions cease, when we no longer carry business cards with a prestigious title?

It's the ultimate act of love and service to do everything possible not to be missed. To be quickly forgotten is hard on the ego, but it's the best bet for our organizations and for our souls.

Antidotes

Thankfully, there are antidotes to the leadership plagues of fear and pride: trust and humility.

Guided by trust and humility, leaders find freedom in exploring their transition. When free from fretting over how they'll be remembered, leaders can have an honest conversation about what it takes to transition well. Simply put, leaders who transition well consider their leadership expendable—in the very best sense of the word.

Anxiety about the future is nothing new, and the prescription Jesus offers is to trust that God will take care of us. Fear of the future dissipates when we believe in God's provision and care. In the most famous sermon in all of history, Jesus tells His disciples:

"Do not worry about your life, what you will eat; or about your body, what you will wear. For life is more than food, and the body more than clothes. Consider the ravens: They do not sow or reap, they have no storeroom or barn; yet God feeds them. And how much more valuable you are than birds! Who of you by worrying can add a single hour to your life? Since you cannot do this very little thing, why do you worry about the rest?"[iii]

Wrestling with fear? Ask God why it is that you don't fully trust Him. To transition well, we need to learn to trust.

Step off the Stage

When Mike Sharrow was transitioning out of a previous role, he wanted to leave on good terms. He tried to make the last thirty days the best of his career. The CEO confronted him to ask why he was pedaling so hard in these final days. It was then when Mike realized that his intentions, while seemingly good, masked a desire to be needed. The CEO proceeded to say, "By pedaling so fast, you're making it all the harder for a new person to step into the role and live up to your level of productivity. When you leave, it will make you feel good and us feel bad." Talk about unanticipated consequences!

Mike was convicted: "It would have been better to work in such a way that the staff would think fondly of me but not notice that I'm gone since they're doing so well without me."

Fast forward to today: When Mike reflects on his biggest success of 2019, it was during C12's National Meeting. While these three days of intense training are typically driven by the CEO, who also offers a State of the Union address, Mike worked hard to minimize his role in the meeting—giving up his spot to allow others the chance to speak and lead. At the end of the conference, a senior leader approached Mike. "It's been a fantastic few days," he shared. "Do you know what stood out to me most? You could have not been here and it would've been just as good." Mike saw it as a tremendous accomplishment.[iv]

Mike reflected, "It can be an ego-satisfying reality to build a business dependent upon you. It makes you feel important. You get validation, identity, and meaning from the thought that the organization cannot live without you. But there's a danger in finding too much significance from being needed. It makes the idea of not being needed scarier and messier for you."[v]

There's an element of "healthy ego" that contributes to a rise into senior positions of leadership.

It says, "I could lead that organization or that department." But it's that very attitude that can undermine a healthy succession. The attributes necessary for a person to receive a promotion could be precisely the same attributes that undermine their ability to pass it on well.

Justin Straight shares, "It can be difficult to let go of the sins that we have come to think are our strengths. They may have contributed to how and why the organization is doing so well. If they're tied to our identity, we're more likely to rationalize them away." He continued, "But God has made us for relationship, and it is only through relationship that His work is accomplished—not through one person or one leader. Leaders can fall in love with the idea that they are mission critical when they should be responding as if the mission is critical."[vi]

Self-centered leaders build culture and programs around their "personality" instead of the mission. There is a shadow on other people as other leaders transition out of the organization or are never given the opportunity to step up and lead. The team and board have difficulty thinking beyond the type of dominant leader they've experienced, even if that leadership style is eroding culture or organizational effectiveness.

Humility for leaders is summarized not by "How little can I make me?" but "How big can I make you?" A humble person understands that it's not about them. It's not about appearing meek or lowly—that is still about our own image management. Humility is about others. The focus is external and seeks the most meaningful way to build others up.

Sandy Schultz, CEO emeritus of The Work-Faith Connection, shares, "Transition is the greatest opportunity to grow in humility. It means giving up the right to be right."[vii]

Leaving a legacy

John Maxwell writes that the natural progression of leadership follows from achievement to success to significance to legacy: achievement comes when you do great things by yourself, success comes when you empower your employees to do great things for you, significance comes from developing leaders to do great things with you, and legacy comes when you put leaders in a position to do great things without you.[viii]

A Kingdom Legacy, rather than a personal legacy, shapes a transition.

In a personal legacy, the story is mostly about us and what we've done. It elevates our name and our leadership, seldomly recognizing other people. In response, people know how great we are. The story cannot continue without us. At the core, a personal legacy places self first.

In a Kingdom legacy, the story is all about what God has done. Jesus is primary, and the story is about God's restoration and redemption. At the core, a Kingdom legacy places God first.

Consider the legacy you're building now. What do you really want people to remember and know after you are gone? You or God? What you did or what God did?

Price Harding, chairman of CarterBaldwin Executive Search, shares, "Think only about the organization and its mission. Do not allow mission-critical decisions to be made in response to the organization's love for [or disdain for] the incumbent. ... Think about the future – five, ten, fifteen years out and hire the person who can best lead to that future."[ix]

No matter how hard we try to fight it or forget it, we all have an expiration date in our leadership. We are finite and grounding ourselves in this reality will help us plan and prepare well for our transition of leadership.

Surrender: I am not what I do.

When Cody Parkey, NFL kicker for the Chicago Bears, missed a 43-yard field-goal attempt, it cost his team a first-round playoff victory. The Bears lost the game by one point to the Eagles, causing the city of Philadelphia to celebrate and Chicago to mourn.

But Cody knew that his identity extended beyond this moment and even beyond his profession. In an interview afterwards, he shared, "I'm disappointed I let the fans, my teammates, and the entire organization down, but I'll continue to keep my head held high because football is what I do. It's not who I am."[x]

While we want to aim for excellence and hope that our blunders are not televised to millions of fans, we do hope to live with the clarity that we have an identity outside of our work. We will do well to rest in our God-given identity and realize that we are not defined by what we do. Daily, we remember that we live as human beings, not human doings, in Christ.

A close friend of mine (Doug) once commented, "I worked very hard to earn a doctorate degree. Yet now that I have it, I will not use it. That is not who I am. My ego fights not being called a 'Doctor of Ministry,' but I am a child of God. Just call me a Christian or a servant or a follower of Jesus."

There is no better way to be known than through our connection to Jesus.

When a leader's title becomes wrapped around their identity, it's no surprise that succession planning is either readily avoided or quickly dismissed. Succession forces us to face the hard questions: Who am I when I leave? Who am I when I don't have the platform of my role? Where am I going after I leave?

In our interviews, the leaders who had had a successful transition were the ones who had spent time and energy thinking about what was next for them. There was a level of anticipation and even excitement about their future. They had considered where they were headed, not just why they were leaving.

A transition requires surrender. It requires a fierce, collective commitment to allow trust, not fear, to drive the process. It replaces ego with humility, vulnerability, honesty, and transparency. It gives space for people to express their fears and disappointments, and it offers freedom to make healthy decisions rooted in the mission.

Let's trust the process, trust each other, and trust God. For "our" organizations were never really "ours," after all. In Deuteronomy 8:17-18, Moses writes, "You may say to yourself, 'My power and the strength of my hands have produced this wealth for me.' But remember the Lord your God, for it is He who gives you the ability to produce wealth, and so confirms his covenant, which he swore to your ancestors, as it is today." The organizations we lead do not belong to us. They are not possessions to cling to but gifts to steward. And in this, there is joy and freedom.

Mike Sharrow comments, "My board asked me to be ready to do succession within two years of starting with the hope that God would afford me over twenty years with the company. They knew that if I started with succession in mind, the organization would be healthier. Once we surrender the mission, knowing it's not 'ours,' we can truly steward the idea of succession with joy."[xi]

Paul Marty has navigated multiple transitions, including transitioning leadership of his private chiropractor business and transitioning the presidency of HOPE International, but he recently shared that the most difficult transition is the one he is currently facing. It's with Tomorrow Clubs, the organization he and his wife founded and have led for over twenty years. "It's not easy to think of someone else taking care of your baby!" he shared. However, in the next breath, he continued, "I know that even in this moment, I'm a steward of the mission. God is the owner, not me."

Paul concluded by sharing, "This organization was never mine."[xii]

ACTION STEPS:

The Mirror: Where is my identity?

1. **Outgoing Leader:** What do you hope happens to the organization after you are gone? Celebrate the future possibilities and trust that God will guide the future. Acknowledge that God has called you to the place you're in and has given you the grace to lead for a limited period of time.

   Make a list of the fears you have when you think about your transition. Mike Sharrow listed his fears about transition and then wrote the truth about his identity and calling in God's economy. He shared with a small group of close friends and his family, letting them speak into the list as well. "Confessing fears kills their power. Unconfessed fear hijacks the vision," he shared.

   Invite colleagues to call you out anytime they see decisions or behaviors that seem to focus primarily on you instead of on the organization and be willing to listen and respond to their feedback.

2. **Incoming Leader:** Be aware of your own fears and pride issues as you enter into the new role.

Reinforce that the mission matters most and acknowledge that you are part of a much bigger story. Knowing that first impressions make a difference, explore symbolic ways to reinforce that you are coming in as a steward and servant, not a king or queen. Seek to honor others by being ready to wash dishes and wash feet.

3. **Board:** Talk through succession planning together as a board. Are there areas where you need to yield to God's leading? Have you made time and space to think and pray about the 10-15 year plan for the organization? Set aside time to pray together, surrendering the process to the Lord and asking for guidance.

4. **Staff:** How might you set an example in trust and humility during a time of leadership transition? Are there ways to serve your peers and colleagues in this time? Make a list of the fears you have when you think about a leadership transition, and brainstorm practical solutions to address them.

Part 2:

PRACTICES

The first part of this book focused on heart posture: prioritizing the mission, identifying the myths, discerning the timing, finding our identity beyond our role, and examining where fear and pride are undermining healthy succession planning. Getting our hearts in the right place is a necessary prelude to a successful transition. It's like stretching before the race.

Developing the right heart postures is a journey, not a checklist. We don't need to master the heart postures before we move to the practices. In fact, we can invite God to continue refining our hearts while engaging the practices that will help guide us through the transition.

In this next section, we have outlined seven key practices that equip leaders to release or receive the mission—to successfully pass the baton in this critical moment.

These seven practices repeatedly surfaced in conversations with leaders who have transitioned to or from an organization.

The specific practices to guide a succession are built from the practices necessary for a successful relay race:

1. Focus on the whole race.
2. Start training now.
3. Create the plan.
4. Listen to the coach.
5. Communicate clearly.
6. Prepare for the handoff.
7. Cheer on the team.

Let's learn from the relay-racers on how to pass the baton and find success in succession.

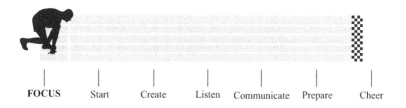

FOCUS   Start   Create   Listen   Communicate   Prepare   Cheer

5

FOCUS ON THE WHOLE RACE

*Home to the world's longest relay race, Japan hosted
the Prince Takamatsu Cup for over fifty years. Participants raced across more than ten different Japanese
cities, covering more than 650 miles as a team.*

*As Brian Lewis writes, the Cup was structured
so that "no single person, no matter how fit, wise, or
determined, could win it on his own."[i]*

While the Prince Takamatsu Cup no longer takes place, there are a host of similar endurance relay races around the world that still display the power of a team working together to run massive distances. Each one of these relay races cover a distance in a time that would be impossible with only one runner.

Runners are to give it their best in individual legs of the race. But ultimately, each runner is focused on a much bigger goal than his or her own leg. At its core, a relay race is a team effort. Relay racers know that they are only one part of a bigger race.

Defining the Mission

As an incoming CEO, Dave[ii] thought his predecessor had prepared him well for the new role he was stepping into. The two met regularly to share history, stories, and the day-to-day systems. As his predecessor began to back away from daily operations, all appeared to be well.

They were on track for a healthy transition until turbulence set in their relationship. Dave's predecessor still served on the board and slowly began using his role to voice dissatisfaction with Dave's leadership. Initially, it was in whispers, but, it was raised louder in board meetings and began to leak beyond the boardroom to individuals supporting the ministry.

In time, Dave realized that the underlying issue wasn't how he was building the team or expanding the operations; rather, it was that the mission was poorly defined. There was a fundamental disagreement about the purpose of the organization. Even though Dave and his predecessor had talked about all of the inner workings of the day-to-day operations, they had not spent time clarifying the heart of the mission.

Initially, they had more clarity about details of the implementation, rather than clarity about the core purpose of the organization. It didn't help that the board also had ambiguity about the mission.

Because the mission touches every part of the organization, even the day-to-day operations were thrown off kilter. The uncertainty in the transition led to a rise of confusion among board members, staff, and even supporters. "What I thought was clear was not," Dave shared candidly. "I misunderstood my role and our team's objectives." Lack of alignment caused havoc for the entire organization.

With the lack of clarity about the mission, over time the outgoing leader only grew more discontent and ended virtually all communications with Dave. Dave tried to resolve the conflict by asking for help from the board chair, but the chair would not step up. Like a ship without a rudder, the organization was drifting.

Unsurprisingly, Dave left the ministry within only a few months.

Of all the considerations involved in succession planning, an unrelenting focus on mission is most critical to a healthy transition. For this reason, missional focus is worth repeating as it is both a heart posture and a practice.

Whether it's packaged in a concise mission statement or outlined in a founding document, the mission is an organization's most valuable asset. It is the purpose—the reason for existence. Mission promotes movement and direction, creating avenues to celebrate the ways God is at work in the world.

What does it mean to steward a mission well? It starts with four words: *It's not about you.* Russ Crosson, chief mission officer at Ronald Blue Trust, calls this the "fundamental punchline."[iii] Rather than owners, missional leaders are simply caretakers of the mission for a given time. And during this time, they may grow the organization, build a team, and invite others to come alongside—all while holding open hands to what God is calling them to as temporary caretakers.

Succession planning is integral to this end. As leaders consider succession planning, they might ask "How will the prospective successor (or next caretaker) understand and embrace the mission? And how can we empower him or her to steward this mission with excellence?" As part of this process, is it essential to engage the full board in clearly defining and championing the mission.

Those leading healthy transitions spot and stop self-centered thinking and ruthlessly adhere to making decisions that place the mission first. After all, the mission—not success in your role—is what matters most. So, we are called to lead in a way that actively prepares for the inevitable future without us. Shine the spotlight on others, give credit, share the microphone, spend time mentoring others, sacrifice personal success for the success of someone else. Put simply, do everything you can to make other people successful.

Paul Park, former executive director of First Fruit Foundation, advises that leaders repeat this phrase to themselves every day: "The mission and the organization are bigger than me." Doing so, he notes, will prevent selfish attitudes—like *Why isn't my vision executed how I want or as fast as I want?*—from becoming primary.[iv]

In successful successions, outgoing and incoming leaders start with the mission, clarifying as needed to provide direction and achieve unity.

Jesus' Mission

We don't need to look further than Jesus for an example of how to live our lives focused on our mission. Jesus' attitude toward mission is modeled in every part of His ministry. When teaching His disciples to pray, Jesus said, "Your Kingdom come, Your will be done, on earth as it is in heaven."[v] Jesus knew His mission and didn't deviate from it. His coming to seek, to save, to love, to heal, to preach, to deliver, and to die for us all flowed from His mission.

When Jesus left Earth and returned to the Father, every disciple knew they had a responsibility to continue the work Jesus had started. And in the years following Jesus' ascension, that motley crew of fishermen, zealots, and tax collectors made an indelible mark on the world for the Kingdom.

Jesus had clarity about His mission and passed it onto others. Could we say the same of ourselves?

Transitioning well begins with a commitment to base all decisions on what is ultimately best for the long-term health of the organization.

The mission matters most.

ACTION STEPS:

Focus on the Whole Race

1. **Outgoing leader:** More than any other time in your tenure, this is the time to share the mission with absolute clarity. Consider meeting with staff and board members to talk through anything that might be too confusing or complicated. Is the organization's purpose (mission) and desired state (vision) crystal clear? Where are there gaps in communication and clarity? Does the approach to finances, staffing, and fundraising point back to the mission? As a gift to the incoming leader, resist the urge to launch new initiatives or projects that cannot be fully accomplished before your exit.

2. **Incoming leader:** Come in with humility and a learning posture. Sit down with the outgoing leader, the board, and the staff to gain clarity on the organization's mission. Understand how the key performance indicators connect to the mission. When stepping into a new role, it can be easy to get excited about all of the possibilities without having full clarity of purpose. Make sure you're taking time to clarify the core mission

before brainstorming innovative approaches for day-to-day operations. Both are important, but they need to be in the right order.

3. **Board:** As a board member, your role is, first and foremost, to safeguard the mission. Is there anything unclear about your core purpose? Before bringing a new leader in, scour the organization's documents to ensure clear and honest messaging about the mission. Start with board documents, by-laws, and policy manuals. Then, look at the website: mission and vision statements, core values, and methodology. When the new leader is hired, invite him or her to work with you to clarify language for anything he or she thinks is unclear. Above all, ensure that you hire someone who is passionate about the mission of the organization.

4. **Staff:** Regularly remind yourself of why you joined the organization. Have there been times that you have been tempted to put yourself ahead of the mission? How might you keep the mission at the forefront?

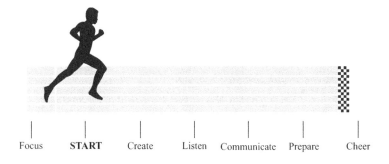

| Focus | **START** | Create | Listen | Communicate | Prepare | Cheer |

6

START TRAINING NOW

When you watch runners walk to the starting line to begin the race, you know this isn't their first time on a track. They have been training for this moment for years. They have woken up early to lace up their shoes when the rest of us were sipping coffee in our PJs. They have chosen green smoothies instead of Co-ca-Cola and salad instead of french fries. They hav-

en't just gone on the occasional run but have modeled consistent training over years.

So when it's race day, they are ready. They have been training for this moment.

For relay-racers, there's an added element of training. Behind a successful baton pass is months of training and practice with their teammates. There are calluses from the baton passes and a familiarity to the sound of the baton slapping their teammate's hands.

They aren't trying to figure it out on race day; they are prepared for this moment.

Planning Early

Over a decade ago, the leadership team at InterVarsity recognized they had a problem. Almost all of their current senior leaders would arrive at retirement age within five to eight years. Knowing this, the board encouraged Alec Hill, then-president, to take active steps in thinking about transition. Just saying "We will transition" aloud helped to remove the psychological barrier.

As part of his succession planning, Alec sought to create a pool of people who could move into senior-level positions across InterVarsity.

Together with Paul Tokunaga, who served as the vice president of strategic ministries at the time,

Alec created a Prospective Senior Leadership Cohort. The goal was to proactively and intentionally prepare rising leaders for senior-level positions and help take the mystery out of advancement. An open nominations process was conducted, and Alec's team collectively selected fifteen InterVarsity staff.

Those chosen for the cohort built relationships with each other—a positive, unintentional byproduct. It was obvious that each leader cared more deeply about the mission and future of InterVarsity than where they would fit.

The Prospective Senior Leadership Cohort took an investment of both time and finances. Alec and each vice president mentored two participants for two years. Funds were raised, so that each person had resources to invest in coaching and training. Of those fifteen prospective senior leaders, seven are vice presidents today. And when Alec was diagnosed with bone marrow cancer, his sudden departure was cushioned by a group of rising leaders who were ready to lead.[i]

Alec and the team at InterVarsity had the ability to look forward, not just one year, but five. They had the wisdom to begin preparing for their transitions years in advance.

When you look at your leadership pipeline, what do you see? Internally, how many candidates are ready and capable to assume your role or other senior leadership positions? If like Alec and the InterVarsity team, that list seems shallow, it's time to do the hard work of preparation. This is an opportunity to invest in a dedicated and committed group of future leaders.

Alec recommends keeping a running list of your top ten to twenty "high potential" future leaders. Curating this list should not simply be the responsibility of one individual but of the entire senior team. Ensure that those identified and invested into are not just individuals similar to the current leader. The healthiest organizations actively and intentionally invest in a diverse team, knowing that a leadership pipeline is stronger with men and women of different backgrounds, races, ethnicities, ages, and leadership styles.[ii]

Of course, organizational capacity building stretches far beyond the leader. It takes into account all aspects of the organization: systems, risk mitigation, finances, strategic planning, board governance, staff development, and more. The organizations most prepared for successions are those who don't procrastinate on building capacity across the entire organization.

InterVarsity's wisdom and advanced planning is uncommon. Mike Sharrow shares: "Most people wait too long to prepare and end up in a rushed circumstantial succession. Delayed planning creates a forced or compromised process."[iii]

Similarly, Tiger Dawson, co-founder and CEO of Edify, concisely summarized, "Lack of advance planning is the number one reason that succession planning doesn't go well."[iv]

Raising up Future Leaders

Like InterVarsity's Prospective Senior Leadership Cohort, Ronald Blue Trust holds a CEO Roundtable where they bring in the top twelve leaders and spend eighteen months pouring into them with leadership and financial training. They, too, realize that leaders are only to lead for a limited amount of time and are committed to transferring the "know-how" and the "know-who."

At Ronald Blue Trust, Russ Crosson's specific role is to train and raise up future leaders. It's important to "give someone else their moment," he says.[v]

This requires "long-term discipline in a short-term world," as Paul Marty describes.[vi] For leaders, this is particularly difficult because we are rewarded primarily for short-term and personal accomplishments—the exact opposite of where we need to focus on succession planning.

The right time to invest in your internal team and ensure there are multiple viable candidates for next-level leadership is today. Perhaps it's time to more intentionally give away your platform and aspects of decision-making, so that others can shine. By intentionally saying no to opportunities, others on the team are empowered to say yes.

You can test the waters and response of others by carefully giving to potential successors some of the responsibilities of your role. Ask them to speak in front of a group that would have been your assignment. Encourage them to write a document others would have expected from you. Invite them to a board meeting to give a report on their work. Increase their visibility and ask them to lead the leadership team in your absence. Then, look and listen for feedback.

Be sure to give clear and candid feedback, too. What do these up-and-coming leaders need to hear to continue growing? Coaching is a critical part of succession planning, especially when there is clearly high potential but specific gaps in knowledge or experience.

Noel Tichy, a management professor at the University of Michigan, asserts that giving ownership of projects to potential successors not only accelerates progress in the organization, but it also evaluates a leader's fit for various leadership positions.[vii]

If there is no obvious internal successor at this point, don't beat yourself up. Keep hiring the best people to do the jobs needed and invest in them. Especially if you start early in your tenure, over time, you will see internal leaders excel.

Identifying the Next Leader

Just like in a relay race, it's simply not enough to start preparing early; it's important to get the right runners on the team. What should leaders look for in potential successors?

For InterVarsity's Prospective Senior Leadership Cohort, Alec and his team examined four criteria in potential leaders: character, competency, experience, and high potential.

For David J. Gyertson, vice president of the Dingman Company, identifying the future leader begins with a CEO profile of the leadership qualities needed in the next season. He suggests asking, "Do we need someone to fulfill our vision or someone to help clarify and refine our vision?" The answer will help the board to name the qualities, qualifications, and passions needed in a successor.[viii]

In his book, *Five Attributes: Essentials of Hiring for Christian Organizations*, Chad Carter outlines the 5Cs of hiring in faith-based organizations.[ix]

1. **Character:** Marked by integrity and spiritual maturity, character is developed through dependence on God; challenges and successes; and daily discipline in prayer, Scripture, and worship. It's far easier to teach competencies than it is to teach character. In fact, a research project on effective theological school presidents concluded that "character is a better predictor of executive leaders' success than credentials and interview performance."[x]

2. **Calling:** Leaders with a sense of calling understand how their personal mission fits into the greater Kingdom mission. Knowing that they are part of something greater than themselves builds humility and unity in how they serve and in how they lead.

3. **Competency:** Competency focuses on the know-how: What skills and abilities do leaders bring to the team? What gaps do they fill in the team or organization? Competent leaders push beyond mediocrity toward excellence.

4. **Chemistry:** In the workplace, chemistry evaluates how well an individual will interact with a team. Does he or she align with the team, culture, and mission?

5. **Contribution:** Character, calling, competency, and chemistry ultimately work together to help boards or hiring teams to assess whether or not a candidate will make a meaningful contribution to the mission. Chad notes, "One of the greatest contributions an individual can make to their organization is to achieve significant results by utilizing the contributions of other people. This means the leader has become a multiplier rather than a single contributor."[xi]

This framework is important for any sort of hiring but even more significant when recruiting for a leadership position. As Buck Jacobs, founder of the C12 Group, advises, "If you notice some warning signs early on with a potential candidate, be careful. Those signs will become even more exaggerated in a leadership position."[xii]

No candidate is perfect, but it is important for the board to ensure that prospective candidates' weaknesses are not in areas that are crucial for the organization's performance.

Considering Culture

Although each organization has its own culture, needs, and priorities, there are some elements that every organization needs to weigh when considering a new CEO.

According to a HireRight study, 26% of employers rely on gut instinct when hiring CEOs.[xiii] Yet, in order to appoint the right CEO for the organization, boards and CEOs must work together to identify the responsibilities and skills necessary for the next-generation leader to succeed.

These responsibilities should be updated annually. Having a current, complete job description is particularly critical if the organization is driven by an especially charismatic or forceful CEO, since their actual skills may be overshadowed by their personality.

Warren Bird, vice president of research and equipping at the Evangelical Council for Financial Accountability notes, "Leaders have long understood that when you need to change the culture, you hire from without, but when you want to reinforce the existing culture, you hire from within."[xiv]

Brian Lewis writes in his book, *Ways of the Relay-Racers*, "In some organizations, leadership succession is more than leadership selection. In some organizations, leadership succession means culture succession."[xv] When it comes to conversations around succession, we are talking about the culture the board wants to preserve, protect, or create.

All board members must be on the same page about culture and the leadership skills that matter most. Rachel Spier Weaver, senior human resources business partner at HOPE International, recommends, "Boards must have agreement on the purpose of the CEO role, a vision for its growth, and clear expectations of delivery."[xvi] As board members clarify these with each other and with the current CEO, the transition process—when it arises—will be less turbulent.

Succession planning hinges on getting the right leader on the team, someone who will positively shape culture and invest in other strong leaders.

Providing Advanced Notice

While opinions vary based on the sector and state of the organization, it is often recommended that the current CEO provide six to nine months notice to the board of directors. In so doing, there is adequate time provided to formally pursue a thoughtful process and search for the successor. Staying on for a limited period of time will also communicate to staff and stakeholders that there is not an unspoken problem.

When preparing to transition from Treetops Collective, the nonprofit she co-founded, Dana Doll remembers, "Given the depth of relationships and belief in the mission, I thought that I would want a long and slow transition. But the reality was that as soon as the new leader was announced, the best way I could care for the organization was to get out of the way."[xvii]

Sometimes, the best way to advance the mission is to quickly make space for the new leader to truly lead.

For thirteen years, I (Doug) had served as an executive pastor with senior pastor, Ed Dobson, at Calvary Church in Grand Rapids, Michigan. God had blessed the ministry and my relationship with Ed. We had a commitment to serve together for life.

But plans changed in the spring of 2003 with Ed's ALS diagnosis.

At that time, Ed's prognosis was a life expectancy of five years. After prayer, tears, and time to think, Ed and I had a serious conversation about the future. Ed was going to transition from his leadership role quickly. Because our gifts and skills balanced so well in our relationship as pastors of Calvary, we both sensed that I should also step down to make space for the new senior pastor to bring in his or her own executive leader.

We concluded that this was a moment for both of us to transition fairly quickly to make space for the new leader. We watched as a new pastor replaced

Ed and brought with him a new executive pastor, replacing me. The church continued, and we were once again reminded that God does provide.

Of course, there are exceptions and times when the current leader leaves or needs to leave immediately, before a new successor is hired. During those situations, the board needs to be strong and work closely with the staff to ensure strong morale and missional focus.

Handling Quick Transitions

Dawson Trotman founded the Navigators ministry as a young adult in the 1930s. With a passion for discipleship, Dawson started training and mentoring high school students. When one of his mentees came and asked him to teach an inquisitive young sailor, Dawson responded simply, "You teach him!" And with that posture, the organization started to grow rapidly. Soon, the sailor had taught his crew, and 125 men aboard the U.S.S. Virginia were growing in Christ and sharing their faith with others—in the middle of World War II. By the end of the war, thousands of people on ships and bases around the world were equipped in God's Word and learning the value of spiritual multiplication. Few ministries have seen as many people come to Jesus out of the aftermath of

World War II.

Dawson was a visionary with an insatiable appetite to share the Gospel. But at just fifty years old, Dawson drowned in a small lake in upper New York state. The tragedy of the evangelist's death hit the headlines, and almost 3,000 people, including Billy Graham, showed up to his funeral.

The leader was gone, but not the mission. In talking about this transition, The Navigators website shared, "The Navigators is Bible-based and Christ-centered, not dependent on a man."[xviii] Since Dawson's death, the Navigators has grown more rapidly than ever before. At the core was a ministry that was reproducible, effective, and contagious. Thanks to Dawson's advanced planning and focus on multiplication and discipleship, the mission continues to thrive to this day.

Few of us get to plan the timing of our succession any more than we get to "plan" a medical crisis or family emergency. But one thing is certain: if you're thinking about succession at the moment when you need a successor, you're too late!

If boards and CEOs care deeply about the mission of their organization, they will start actively planning for succession long before they think it will be a reality. Beyond a specific succession plan, the most important aspect of preparation comes down to a culture of leadership development.

Preparing for the Next Generation

Preparing for future generations of leadership starts now.

When I (Doug) was touring the land of the Bible, I was intrigued by the number of unfinished homes in Cana and Nazareth. The first two stories were completed, and with clothes drying on balconies and people going in and out of the homes, it was obvious they were occupied. When I asked our guide why so many had rebar and partially-constructed roofs, he laughed and shared how they were preparing for the next generation. "When their sons or daughters get married, they will complete their living space on the third floor."

There's a similar lesson in the tamarisk tree. If we're not careful, we might skip over this minute detail in Genesis 21. Shortly after Abraham arrives in Beersheba, he plants a tamarisk tree and calls on the name of the Lord.[xix] Tamarisk trees do not sprout up within a few years like aspens or maple trees. Rather, they take eighty years to grow.[xx] Those who plant tamarisk trees don't plant it for themselves nor for their children, but for their grandchildren. Their grandchildren are the ones who will enjoy the work and cultivation of the tree.

In Abraham's case, planting a tamarisk tree meant that He trusted in the promises of God so much that he, his children, and his grandchildren would stay in the land for a long time. In the case of today's leaders, figuratively planting a tamarisk tree means that we are serving a mission beyond ourselves, planning well for generations to come. When we plant a tamarisk tree, we do so for others.

What are the things you're doing today in leadership that will live beyond you?

Later in Scripture, King David made preparations for his successor, Solomon, to build God's temple. In 1 Chronicles 28, David declares, "I had it in my heart to build a house as a place of rest for the ark of the covenant of the Lord, for the footstool of our God, and I made plans to build it. But God said to me, 'You are not to build a house for my Name … Solomon your son is the one who will build my house and my courts.'"[xxi] Submitted to God, David gave Solomon all of the plans and instructions the Holy Spirit had given him for the temple's construction. He empowered Solomon to fulfill the vision.

Like Abraham and David, how can we think long term about our missions and visions, starting to prepare now for fulfillment years down the road?

ACTION STEPS:

Start Training Now

1. **Outgoing leader:** Annually, give the board the names of five people who could do your job well. These are people whom you believe fit the profile of a successful leader. Of course, be sure to keep this list between you and the board, but review this list and talk about succession planning with the board every year. (The right people when you created this list might not be the right people in the current season.) Find ways to regularly give opportunities, especially for internal staff, to develop and grow into leadership roles.

   Consider cataloging how much time you're spending investing in others (internally and externally) you think could be your successor. (If the answer is zero, the only way to go is up!) Create an emergency succession plan as well and review it annually. In the event of a sudden change, the organization should have an emergency plan that goes into effect immediately. Well in advance of your transition, do the difficult work of readying the organization for your departure.

2. **Incoming Leader:** Bathe the transition in prayer. When I (Doug) accepted the role to be the CEO of Marketplace Chaplains, I went to my coach, Steve Douglass, who serves as the president of Cru. I asked what my wife and I should do before we moved to Dallas to begin the role. Steve quietly responded, "Just one thing, Doug: Pray like you never prayed before." I created a new prayer list, my longest ever. I developed an entirely new daily routine with more time for prayer than ever before. It has shaped my heart and life as a leader. The incoming leader takes ownership and personal command of readying his or her heart for the new role. Lean into God for His perspective and guidance, practicing the "abiding" in John 15, as needed.

3. **Board:** Chuck Shinn, president of Builder Partnerships, notes that when it comes to succession planning, "The big mistake that companies make is that they assume things will happen without putting together a game plan."[xxii] It is the responsibility of the board to prioritize succession planning, and it must be an annual conversation, at least, with the current leader.

4. **Staff:** Consider how a leadership transition could affect your role or your team. Would a transition create a void on your team? If so, how could you step up with support to fill that gap? Take time to pray and plan accordingly. Consider talking with the human resources team, as necessary.

7

CREATE THE PLAN

My (Peter's) sister-in-law Kelly Steinweg is one of those insane ultramarathon runners. Immediately after completing a fifty-mile race in Steamboat Springs, Colorado, that included over 7,000 feet of elevation gain, she commented, "That was awesome!" In the highly unlikely scenario that I would ever choose to run or finish such a race, I'm quite certain that "awesome" would not be among the first words out of my mouth.

It's not just this Colorado race; Kelly competes in long-distance relay races, including the Hood to Coast relay, known as the "Mother of all Relays." This 199-mile race begins at Mt. Hood in Oregon and finishes at the Pacific Ocean, in a town appropriately named Seaside.[i]

This is what she does for fun with her friends.

Preparing for this race goes beyond the personal training. In a twelve-person team, you have to be prepared physically and logistically. This means planning flights and arrival times in Portland, preparing the vans and food for the course, and coordinating sleep schedules (as the race will take close to thirty hours). It also involves thinking through which legs each person will run, based on the terrain and distance of each leg, and where each team member will meet to pass on the baton to the next runner.

You don't finish the race if you're unwilling to put in the important work of planning.

Even if it's not a long-distance race, all relay racers understand the need to plan. Who will run each leg? Where will we pass the baton? Which technique will we use? Which hand does the incoming runner have the baton in, and which hand will I receive it in? With only a twenty-meter exchange zone for one runner to release the baton and the next runner to take *hold of it, there isn't much time to get it right. Relay racers understand the need to have a clear plan in place before the race begins.*

Prayerfully Prepared

When Dan Wolgemuth was in the final interview process for becoming the president at Youth for Christ (YFC) USA, a YFC board member asked how long he would want to serve, if he was given the position. Off the cuff, he said ten years. After more consideration, interviews, and meetings, the board invited him to join as the president of YFC. Just a few years ago, at year nine, the newly-elected board chair prompted him to ask the Holy Spirit about his next step. He and his wife, Mary, committed to six more years in 2014. And in the fall of 2018, the board talked more seriously about succession planning.

At the start of 2020, Dan announced his plans to step down from YFC. He shared, "I will step down with joy and confidence that God has His hand on this mission and on its new leader."[ii]

What stands out wasn't just the clear communication between Dan and his board but the willingness to thoughtfully and prayerfully create the plan of his transition.

As part of his communication process, he

shared an illustration from the Tour de France, where the best cyclists from around the world come together for a twenty-three-day competition. The teams often clump together in large groups, with a *domestique* in the lead. The domestique, translated "servant," is the cyclist who rides in the front, pressing against headwinds and navigating the pack. As the servant, the domestique protects and guards the team, making their work more efficient.[iii]

"I've never been the leader of YFC," Dan concluded in his presidential update. "I've only been the domestique."[iv]

Dan had clarity that it was time for his transition and got to work ensuring that he crafted a plan to honor the organization's mission. This was done in close connection and conjunction with his board.

Board Engagement

The plan of succession requires the full engagement of the board. It's at the moment of transition that you discover the health of this relationship between the board and the CEO. This relationship is crucial in navigating succession planning.

Phil Clemens summarizes, "The board has two primary roles: protecting the mission and hiring the CEO. Succession planning is one of the two critical roles of a board, yet we often don't spend sufficient time in this significant role."[v]

Conversations on succession planning aren't easy or comfortable for anyone. Board members often don't like to face the possibility of disruption brought on by significant change within the organization. And this is a topic where CEOs must embrace courage and humility to look beyond their own tenure. You can't begin creating a plan for succession if you're unwilling to have conversations about succession planning.

Selecting the new leader is the board's responsibility, but governance experts believe the CEO should be an active participant in the process during the preparatory stages. In most healthy settings, the CEO is the person most likely to have deep knowledge of the role's demands, a clear sense of the organization's direction, and an extensive network of qualified contacts and colleagues. It makes sense that he or she would have helpful and unique insight into next-generation leadership that would be valuable to the board.

However, in most settings, the outgoing CEO may best refrain from personal engagement in the actual search process of engaging with future candidates. Phil Clemens shares, "The current leader can be a resource but should not pick the successor."[vi]

It can be intimidating to discuss a succession plan, especially when you don't envision your transition in the relatively near future. Still, it's a healthy habit to create the plan in advance of when you think it will be necessary.

The board and the CEO together have a responsibility to create the plan, including the timeline of how to talk to stakeholders in the transition process. As the board and the CEO communicate with each other about the leadership shift, it is essential that the CEO corresponds with staff about the transition as well. In short, leaders should work to minimize surprises throughout the leadership change.

Create the Process

When Bruce Dingman's pastor decided to step down from his role, the elder team knew it would be difficult news for the congregation to hear. The pastor had founded the church and brought God's word to the congregation weekend after weekend. And the intimate, deeply spiritual relationships he carried with the congregants made the thought of transition even more difficult.

With sensitivity to the congregation, the elder team leaned into what congregants were feeling and provided regular updates about the search process.

Knowing that the process would take time, they didn't rush (and, they made sure to communicate that, too).

The elders appointed a search committee of nine individuals, diverse in age, gender, and roles. Each person committed to making a decision based not on their own preferences, but on what would be best for the church. Not only that, but the search committee held several focus groups to get input from the various constituents about what they'd like to see in the next senior pastor. Developing buy-in for the process also helped people to adjust to the thought of changing leadership.

Working with the outgoing pastor, the chair helped the pastor to "disappear for six months to a year." It was agreed he would start a new ministry that would be separate from the church and function outside of the geographical area. This new ministry helped him to find something to retire *to*, as he continued to use his strengths and giftings to serve the Lord.

The church was able to navigate this important season because of the clear plan put in place.[vii]

How about you? Do you have a clear process that is understood by all key constituents and will guide you through this important time?

ACTION STEPS:

Create the Plan

1. **Outgoing Leader:** Review the succession plan—both the emergency short-term plan as well as the longer-term recruitment process and timeline. Examine the plan with the board for any gaps, particularly in communication to key stakeholders. Ensure you have a plan for internal staff development and investing in emerging leaders.

2. **Incoming Leader:** Review the succession plan with the board and the outgoing leader. Ask probing or clarifying questions, as needed. The fewer surprises, the better! Connect with the board for any concerns throughout the process.

3. **Board:** Create both an emergency succession plan and a longer-term succession plan, including clear communications to all stakeholders. (For a suggested timeline and list of steps, see Appendix 4.) When the time to transition does arise, the amount of time you need to spend together as a board will increase. Greg Barnes adds, "Boards can increase the healthiness of

transition simply by being clear about what it means to govern versus operate the organization." An incoming CEO's success is contingent upon the board's understanding and adherence to healthy governance.[viii]

4. **Staff:** Recognize the void a transition may create and be willing to step up and respond. Of course, all of us have questions: What will the leader do or not do? What will a leadership transition mean for my role? As many details are ironed out during the search process, the leadership team may not have all of the answers right away, so be willing to ask questions with open hands and offer grace.

8

LISTEN TO THE COACH

We ignore the advice of coaches to our own peril. Not heeding their advice can be a costly move for the runner and the team.

The best runners know that they need a coach by their side. They rely on the training plans and preparation. On race day, the coach guides and cheers them on from the sidelines, offering experience and expertise.

The Guides

Long-time strength and conditioning coach of the Boston Celtics, Bryan Doo knows what it looks like to help athletes perform at their highest level. For fifteen years, he worked with athletes on the best basketball team in the NBA, in my (Peter's) extremely biased opinion.

Doo didn't just help players with specific workouts; he worked with them, so they could understand how to perform at their highest potential. To improve areas of specific vulnerability or injury, he contextualized each workout plan to the players. Celtics' point guard, Marcus Smart, said, "If whatever [Doo] was doing didn't work for you, he would find a way that made it work for you."[i] From planning intense workouts to teaching players how to rest, Doo equipped the team to be physically and mentally prepared for games.

From Harvard University teams to the NBA, Doo has trained all kinds of athletes. When I was in college, I had the privilege of experiencing his intense workouts. Doo is world class at what he does. His competency and guidance helps athletes to perform at their highest level, even while recovering from injuries.

Athletes commonly have different coaches for different aspects of their game. From a strength and conditioning coach to a mental coach to a nutrition coach to a life coach to a technical skills coach, athletes know there is wisdom in listening to specific experts.

But coaching isn't just for athletes; it's for each of us. In succession planning, why would we skip the coaching and try to figure it all out on our own?

In our interviews with leaders who successfully navigated their transition, each one walked through this time guided by coaching from others. They actively sought out wise, trusted leaders to help them navigate this time. These were people who demonstrated the capacity to help navigate the emotional, operational, and spiritual dynamics of a transition.

None of us are ever too seasoned, too wise, or too old to have a coach. Look around, pray, and invite someone you trust who can coach you.

Steve Douglass is a personal friend and ministry coach for me (Doug). For nearly five years, I would sit in his office with my list of questions. His sage advice guided me through my leadership journey. When the call came from a headhunter to consider a role at Marketplace Chaplains, I sought out Steve's advice. He became my prayer warrior. He asked me the tough questions I wasn't always willing to ask myself. He was a voice of calm in a whirlwind of unsteady emotions and uncertainties, and he guided me safely through the process. While I had made a few transitions before this one, this time seemed very different with an inordinate number of unknowns. Without Steve, the process would have been very lonely, and I wouldn't have transitioned nearly as well.

A Constellation of Coaches

When I (Peter) first stepped into my role at HOPE, I was twenty-nine years old and knew that there were significant gaps in my knowledge and experience. With both my career and family starting to grow, I needed help in business, fundraising, marriage, faith, and more.

Around this time, I was given a copy of *Connecting*, written by Paul Stanley and J. Robert Clinton. The book advocated for building different kinds of mentoring relationships: upward mentoring (people to learn from), peer co-mentors (people to learn alongside), and mentees (people to mentor). At its core, "constellation mentoring" broke down areas of growth. Instead of looking for one super-charged mentor, constellation mentoring focused on learning from a variety of different people. It focused on building a coalition of guides.

Seeking to grow in my faith, for example, I pursued a spiritual mentor—someone rooted in Christ with spiritual depth. Eager to learn how to scale an organization, I searched for the most successful entrepreneur I could find and asked if he would invest in me. This constellation model of mentoring led me to find strong mentors in fundraising, microenterprise development, and more. While I originally asked these mentors for a two-year commitment, all have become lifelong friends. Their wisdom and insight empowered me to try and speak into the lives of others in the same way they had spoken into mine.

There may be no time that mentorship is more important than in succession planning. In your constellation of mentors, find a guide for your succession. There are many who have navigated their own transitions and understand the right heart preparations and practices to mentor you in this transition. As Proverbs 15:22 reminds us, "Plans fail for lack of counsel, but with many advisers, they succeed."

Part of this coaching is because transition includes grief. The outgoing leader will likely experience a level of loss that is important to process with others. When David Norman transitioned from Erskine College without certainty on where he would go next, he described that the transition felt like a "death."[i] He recognized the benefit of walking through this time with friends and mentors to help process this grief.

During a transition, the board may also benefit from an executive coach to guide them through the selection process, whether that is through a search firm or an experienced leader. For many, this is a good reason why external firms are recruited, tapping into the wisdom and experience of those who have helped navigate succession in a variety of contexts.

Succession is a moment when we are wise to walk with others, learning from their successes and failures.

In many ways, that has been part of the gift of writing this book. We have been given the opportunity to intentionally engage with leaders and friends who have navigated their own transitions. We've learned from their experiences of what worked well, and sometimes more importantly, what didn't.

Remember: The journey of leadership transition is not one that you should walk alone.

ACTION STEPS:

Listen to the Coach

1. **Outgoing Leader:** The best leaders know their need for coaching. Who is walking with you as you plan and prepare for your exit? Examine at least three areas to grow and ask specific expert coaches to mentor you in those areas. This is a time to talk with wise advisors and guides. Similarly, consider what coaching resources will be available to your successor.

2. **Incoming Leader:** Seek out a coach (or several) now; don't wait until it's time to transition. Examine at least three areas to grow and ask expert coaches to mentor you in those areas.

3. **Board:** Identify external support or an external facilitator to help create and guide the organization through the leadership transition. If you're considering a search firm, take a look at Appendix 3.

4. **Staff:** Ask yourself: Who is walking with me right now? What voices am I allowing to influence my thinking? Seek out a mentor or a coach, especially one who models and encourages a Kingdom posture.

Focus   Start   Create   Listen   **COMMUNICATE**   Prepare   Cheer

9

COMMUNICATE CLEARLY

Runners know how to communicate. When preparing for the handoff—especially a blind handoff—incoming runners will literally shout "stick!" to let the outgoing runners know that the baton is coming.

Relay racers know that communication is an integral part of the strategy. They communicate well with their team, especially in the moment of the baton pass.

Speaking the Language of Succession

Chris Crane, co-founder and former CEO of Edify, had experienced multiple transitions throughout his career in both the for-profit and nonprofit sectors. He understood how important this moment was both for the individual leaving and for the person assuming the new role.

Just a few months after launching Edify, Chris and his co-founder, Tiger Dawson, started planning for succession five years down the road. At the time, Chris was the CEO and Tiger, while co-founder, was the president and reported to Chris. Every year, they checked in with each other on the subject of transition and sought the Lord for His timing. After five years, Chris sensed a call to lead for a few more years. "Tiger never pushed to be CEO. He said he was in no hurry and would trust the Lord to reveal the right time," Chris shared.

At their annual check-in a few years later, Chris sensed that they should start putting the succession plan in motion. He cared deeply for the mission but felt a call to step down and let Tiger grab the baton. Together with their wives, Chris and Tiger earnestly prayed over the succession plan and the right timing to activate it.

After several months of prayer, Chris and Tiger sensed a transition at the end of Edify's next fiscal year. They shared their direction with the board of directors, who were enthusiastic about the plan. With advice from an executive recruiter, Chris and Tiger informed the staff of the transition at Edify's annual global staff meeting, eight months before the transition was to take place. (They believed an announcement less than six months beforehand may have suggested that something was wrong.)

"Staff were very enthusiastic over the prospect of Tiger becoming CEO. In fact, I wondered if they were too enthusiastic about Tiger replacing me," Chris laughed.

When Chris transitioned a few months later, he celebrated the moment with a physical passing of a relay-race baton to Tiger. There was no question that this was the moment of transition. In front of family, friends, staff, and donors, Chris shared with Tiger, "I've loved my role, but I know that you are the best person to lead in this next season."

Reflecting on this transition, Tiger shared, "Chris gets all the credit for the successful succession. His mission-first and servant attitude models what a healthy transition should look like."

At Edify's annual leadership summit, they had

a similar moment of symbolically passing the baton. Using powerful imagery, they wanted to make sure that each stakeholder group fully understood the significance of this transition.

Ensuring proper communication with the board, staff, and donors, they also met together with their highly-engaged supporters to ensure that the communication handoff was clear and well received. Systematically, they considered all the stakeholders who would be impacted by this transition and implemented a thorough plan to communicate clearly.

David J. Gyertson shared that the biggest misstep he has seen in succession planning is inadequate communications to key stakeholders about the why, how, and progress of transition.[i]

Three years after the successful transition, Chris reflected, "I loved being the CEO; now I love not being the CEO even more. Tiger has truly taken Edify to heights that I would not have envisioned. I have such joy from the transition going so smoothly and Tiger leading so well."[ii] He proceeded to share that transitions should happen sooner rather than later if there's an ideal, internal leader ready to step into the role.

Staff Communication

"Leaders are communicators," shares Chris Horst, chief advancement officer at HOPE International.[iii] During the months when HOPE responded to the COVID-19 pandemic, Chris stepped in to lead by example and provided clear and consistent communication to the global team. This clarity helped the organization navigate the crisis in ways that strengthened the culture and provided much-needed clarity about priorities and plans.

Of course, the principle of clear communication applies beyond pandemics; it applies in leadership transitions, too. This is a moment when the leaders and board need to excel as communicators. Even some of the most well known corporations do not always communicate clearly in the moment of transition.

After fourteen years leading one of the largest media conglomerates worldwide, Robert Iger transitioned out of his role as CEO of Walt Disney Company in February 2020. And Bob Chapek, who managed Disney's parks and resorts, was immediately named his successor.

But the news came as a shock to Disney staff. In fact, employees only received an internal email about the leadership transition over an hour after Disney sent out a press release. One senior executive at Disney said blatantly, "No one knew this was coming."[iv]

Robert had stated his plans to retire in 2021, but many in the company didn't know what to expect, especially since he had announced and delayed his retirement four separate times over the past ten years. During that time, several internal potential successors left the company, including Tom Staggs, former chief operating officer.[v]

Change of any kind can be difficult, but a change in leadership can be especially challenging, even causing fear and anxiety for staff members. In general, people prefer for things to remain the same, even if they're less than ideal.

Russ Debenport, who leads Strategy for the People, coaches nonprofit leaders in organizational change management. He notes that clear communication is the starting point for change. For leaders introducing change, he recommends building awareness and general knowledge about the change before sharing any detailed information.[vi] This process helps individuals to lean into the change first and be open to the details and timelines later.

"People see change as loss," Russ says.[vii] Empathizing with and understanding the concerns of staff will be a motivator to do everything possible to communicate clearly throughout the process.

Anne Mulcahy, CEO of Xerox, shares, "One of the things we often miss in succession planning is that it should be gradual and thoughtful, with lots of sharing of information and knowledge and perspective, so that it's almost a non-event when it happens."[viii]

Communicate to All Stakeholders

Knowing that a transition causes uncertainty, leaders of the most successful transitions actively plan and consider all stakeholder groups, including program beneficiaries, staff, partners, and donors.

Scott Messner, pastor of strategic initiatives at Calvary Church in Lancaster, notes that it's critical to communicate the transition to every stakeholder group, so there's no confusion. To do so "honors the integrity of the mission and the culture of the organization."[ix]

Pay attention to the external stakeholders, including the supporters of the mission. These generous and engaged people have been investing in the mission through their time, talent, and treasure. I (Doug) am a raving fan and long-term supporter of Youth for Christ. It is through that ministry that I surrendered my life to Jesus. While I have no official connection to the ministry outside of my support, I care deeply about the mission and am eager to feel like I'm on the "inside" when it comes to leadership transitions.

Many supporters may feel a sense of deep loyalty to the leader. When the leader departs, there can be a loss of connection, especially if other relationships were not cultivated. Transitioning well means communicating with stakeholders in a way that deepens loyalty to the mission even more than the connection to the leader.

For example, at a recent annual ministry dinner, the spouse of a board member commented, "We have given to this mission for over twenty-five years and tonight was the first I realized what they do." What changed? Instead of a focus on the leader, the evening focused on the mission and stories of personal transformation. To transition well, leaders must be in the practice of regularly communicating about the mission and impact.

I (Doug) will never forget bringing three business couples together for dinner at our house. I shared with them a vision for training urban pastors with theological education. I simply said, "I don't know what to do. Would you help me?" Their response exuded excitement, and I commissioned them to meet without me and design a solution to the problem. One month later, they shared their report with me. It was brilliant ... and costly. When I saw the price tag, I noted, "We don't have the funds for this." They responded, "We know, but we do." And, they did. As leaders actively communicate about the mission, stakeholders can be drawn into the things that matter most.

ACTION STEPS:

Communicate Clearly

1. **Outgoing Leader:** Moments of change can bring feelings of grief, loss, and even fear to the surface. Give yourself time to mourn the losses you will experience, and consider sharing them with a trusted friend. Whenever possible, infuse internal and external communications with messages of hope. Share your confidence in the new leader with an enthusiastic endorsement, perhaps during a public commissioning ceremony.

2. **Incoming Leader:** Craft communications built on gratitude—for the organization, its mission, its history, and its leadership—and hope for the future.

   Take time to get to know and communicate with various stakeholders. Begin praying over every name. (Yes, every name.) During your first 90 days, there will be nothing more important than getting to know these individuals. Make time in your calendar to schedule in-person meetings and meals with staff, board members, and other stakeholders. Keep the agenda simple. With a focus off of yourself, ask questions that strengthen the relationship: What is your story? Could you tell me about your family? What energizes you about this mission? How can I pray for you?

3. **Board:** Own this moment of transition by developing a timeline for the communication process and prayerfully walk the organization through it. Once a new leader is selected, be hospitable in communication. Consider setting up meetings with stakeholders and gatekeepers, dreaming together about the future, or setting aside time of corporate prayer. Whenever possible, err on the side of transparent and thorough communication. Unnecessary secrets erode trust.

4. **Staff:** Consider what leaders have communicated well in the succession planning process. Is there anything you still have questions about? If you do have questions, ask gently. Know that this is often a time of both joy and grief for the transitioning leader.

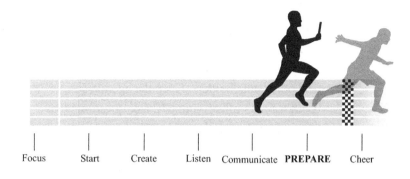

Focus | Start | Create | Listen | Communicate | **PREPARE** | Cheer

10

PREPARE FOR THE HANDOFF

For relay racers, the baton handoff is the most critical moment of the race. A runner could achieve a personal record, but if the handoff is sloppy, the race could quickly be lost.

In the 2019 World Athletics Championship, China's team fumbled the baton in the final handoff of the 4x100 women's relay in what is known online as

"the worst baton pass ever."[i] Teammates Kong Lingwei and Ge Manqi overstepped the exchange zone and tried to pass the baton too late. After racing back to the exchange zone, the teammates spent a few seconds arguing over who should carry the baton before one of them grabbed it and ran toward the finish line, finishing twenty-three seconds after the second-to-last place team.[ii]

What does it look like to prepare well for a baton handoff? It means that when the outgoing runner sees the incoming runner coming down the stretch, they get in their lane, so they're lined up to continue running straight. Then, well before receiving the baton, they start running. The goal is to match each other's speed and keep up the momentum for the handoff. If the person receiving the baton does not begin running soon enough, the incoming runner crashes into them. If they go too fast or too early, they have to slow down to not miss the exchange zone. In sprint relays, the speed matching in the exchange is a critical difference.

Once they've matched the speed, outgoing runners will stretch their hand back to receive the baton. For a very, very short time, both the incoming runner and the outgoing runner will have a hand on the baton. If the incoming runner lets go too soon, the baton falls. If the outgoing runner doesn't take a firm grasp, the baton falls. And of course, when the baton falls, it's not just those two that lose; it's the entire team.[iii]

Leaders Clean Up their Messes

In 2017, Danielle Edwards rented her home in Mount Rainier, Maryland, to three women on AirBnB. The women told her that they were looking for a place to stay for a quiet weekend together.

But when Danielle pulled into the driveway at the end of the weekend, she found something she did not expect. There were Jell-O shot cups littered on the front lawn. Her hardwood floors were scratched. There were footprints on the walls, and trash and vomit littered her once-clean home. The damages totaled over $10,000.[iv] There was a serious lack of respect for the homeowner.

We would never do anything so egregious as leaving a mess behind, right?

However, when it comes to transitions, it's easy to leave our own version of footprints on the wall. Are there staffing decisions that you should have made? Are there difficult programmatic decisions you've avoided? Are you steering clear of some hard conversations in an effort to be liked?

Leaders that navigate healthy successions do

everything possible to set up their successor for success. This includes not delaying the difficult decisions that you know your successor will have to address.

If the outgoing leader does not clean up the mess, this could be a moment for the board to have the courage to help. There might be tough decisions about staff who need to transition, budgets that need revisions, policies that need to be created or deleted, old systems and structures that need to be replaced. Involving the board in these decisions, however, is far less ideal than the previous leader preparing to leave the organization in a state of health.

McKinsey and Company states it simply: "Departing chief executives can leave their companies in the best possible shape by embracing tough decisions rather than leaving them for the incoming CEO.[v]

Please don't leave a mess for your successor. Not only is that unloving, it may create an unhealthy environment to move the mission forward. Instead of the incoming leader being able to focus on people, mission, vision, and strategy, they are left with a litany of problems that will consume their early days.

Shortly after Katy[vi] took a new role, she realized that there were several staff transitions that were required. Within her first three months, she had to let five staff go—not exactly the warm welcome she had anticipated. A spouse of one of the employees sent a scathing letter—not exactly the type of mail Katy was hoping for during her first few months. Worst of all, when she addressed these transitions with the previous leader, it was evident that this came as no surprise. The previous leader knew these difficult decisions were required, but because of friendships, he hadn't made the tough decisions. Katy shared, "I really wish that these difficult decisions were addressed before I started."

Successful succession requires the outgoing leader and the board to confront the difficult decisions that will help set the successor up for success.

Mike Sharrow comments, "The ideal is that there are no surprises when the new leader joins. For the previous leader, this means having the dangerous conversations now and resolving any organizational drama."[vii] In addition to preparing the staff and board for the change, Mike recommends sharing candidly through a SWOT analysis of the organization, taking into account underlying fears, concerns, and any hidden landmines.[viii]

Part of preparing for this transition includes exploring if all current responsibilities of the exiting leader should be transferred to the new leader. Perhaps this is a time to delegate certain responsibilities to other leaders within the organization who are ready for expanded roles or increased responsibility. This step may help set up the new leader for success.

In a similar situation to Katy's, Stephen[ix] had just stepped into a new executive role. Everyone was excited for this "new day" for growth, empowerment of staff, and "house cleaning." But after a short analysis, Stephen discovered from the staff and outsider constituents that one long-term staff person needed to be removed. One board member even acknowledged, "Jill should never have been hired. We have carried Jill along over the years out of benevolence and a bit of entitlement."

Despite the clarity that it was time for Jill to transition out of the organization, this situation became an embittered battle for nearly two years. After copious records, long discussions, and opportunities to make adjustments, nothing more could be done. When Jill was removed from her position, the current staff applauded Stephen but the former leadership did not. It was two years of sideways energy—and an unnecessary welcome to an unsuspecting leader.

Mario Zandstra once asked a former CEO if he wanted the baton passed back. When asked why, Mario responded candidly, "Because you are meddling in the ministry."[x] The previous leader hadn't ever let go of the batton, hindering Mario from accelerating in the race.

These situations stand in stark contrast to Pastor Ed Dobson. When Ed discovered that his terminal disease would require him to step aside from this role, he spent time asking God what it would take to transition well. As part of this process, he knew that there were bridges that needed to be repaired, so he made a list of people he knew he had hurt or offended during his years of ministry and life. He called or visited with them one by one in an effort to right the wrongs of the past. He renewed relationships, repaired the reputation of the organization, and helped to ensure that the new pastor would be able to move forward without being burdened by the past. He did what he needed to do, knowing there was no other time to do it.[xi]

Coasting is a Crime

Bob Merritt served as the senior pastor of Eagle Brook Church in Minneapolis for almost three decades before transitioning out of his role. Under his leadership, the church grew from 300 to over 20,000 people! In announcing his succession to the congregation, he shared, "I want to hand off the baton when I'm running at full speed so that the whole team wins."[xii]

Preparing well for the handoff means refusing to coast. After years of hard work, there's a temptation to believe that you've earned it and can take it easy. But it's simply not true—nor is it helpful for the organization at large.

In their article, "Making the Most of the CEO's Last 100 Days," Christian Caspar and Michael Halbye explain that "continuing to act as CEO until the very last day boosts the odds of leaving a company in the best shape possible and strengthening the legacy of the departing leader."[xiii]

Outgoing leaders who refrain from making major decisions or try to avoid stepping on the toes of the incoming leader may cause unintentional harm toward the incoming CEO. On the other hand, outgoing leaders who work just as diligently on their last 100 days as they did their first will be more likely to give the incoming CEO several advantages, including operating momentum, a strong management team, and a clean slate.

Caspar and Halbye recommend that outgoing CEOs create a priority list for their final 100 days that is done in concert with their leadership team. Use these days to analyze strategic shifts, personnel decisions, and operational momentum.

Make every day count; don't coast. It will be

a gift to you, your successor, stakeholders, and the entire organization.

Transfer Trust

In conversations with Sandy Schultz, we find our gaze constantly turned upward. Her approach to succession planning is no different. "Don't miss the spiritual growth God has for you in this season," she shared. "Embrace transition as part of your spiritual growth journey."

When Sandy began to transition out of her role as CEO at The WorkFaith Connection, she was excited for the new CEO, Anthony Flynn, to take the organization to new heights. And, she wanted to make sure that the staff could get excited, too, without feeling disloyal to her.

To transfer trust, Sandy started reducing the number of hours she worked in the office each week. With a new leader in the office, she sought to set Anthony up for success, empowering him to make the key decisions and respond to raised questions or concerns. Sandy shared, "We're not trying to limit God to what He has done in the past. We're making space for Him to do new things through the new leader."

If staff did turn to her for comfort, she knew she had a bigger responsibility to point them to God and the work that He was doing in and through the organization. It's His ministry, after all.

Sandy reminded us that even if succession looks different than planned—like an unexpected transition—there's still a way to do it well. "Stop wrestling, and rest in the sovereignty of God," she concluded.[xiv]

Picking Up the Baton

Aside from keeping a firm grip on the baton, a runner's priority in the handoff is to keep momentum. If an outgoing runner is not at the same speed as the incoming runner, the entire team slows down. To maintain momentum during a leadership transition, McKinsey and Company recommend that the new leader focus on four priorities: transition, timing, building, and communicating.[xv]

1. In the *transition* phase, a leader reflects on the context of his or her transition. For external hires, especially, context is critical for understanding the history, board structure, governance, and mission of the organization. It's also advised to view this context through the eyes of other stakeholders. During this phase, the new leader draws up his or her initial set of priorities and intended transition outcomes.

2. During the *timing* phase, a leader determines how to move forward in his or her new role with specific transition goals. Harvard Business Review reports that 80% of CEO appointees have never served in a chief executive role before. [xvi] This phase encourages new leaders to determine how to manage their new agenda and time, develop a process for selecting a top team, and establish ground rules for their own work-life balance.

3. In the *building* phase, leaders commit to creating relationships with the board members, staff, supporters, and more. Since there are many relationships worthy of a new CEO's time, it might be helpful to map out who you'll contact and when. Paul Park suggests going on a listening campaign and speaking with every major stakeholder. Without bringing any sort of prescription to the meeting, ask them why they're connected to the mission and what matters most to them. This not only builds relationship but helps new leaders understand how their stakeholders see the mission.

4. Lastly, the *communication* phase encourages new leaders to consider internal and external communication plans. Will you be personally

visible and accessible or stick to more of a delegation approach? What platforms will you use to leverage presence and reach? What themes are most important to tell the organization's story? During this time, a new CEO might establish a plan for receiving balanced feedback and information as well.[xvii]

With these four priorities in sight, a new leader is better equipped to grasp the baton and maintain momentum.

Will we have the courage and spiritual maturity to prepare well for the handoff? To do the difficult work of preparing the organization for the incoming leader?

ACTION STEPS:

Prepare for the Handoff

1. **Outgoing leader:** When you see the ending point on your horizon, do whatever possible to finish well. Mark Linsz shares that there is a correlation between how you finish your career and how happy you are in retirement. When he was planning for his transition from Bank of America, he committed to four concrete goals: develop

a strong team, find a successor, work to the day you leave (no coasting), and thank people.[xviii]

Start with introspection and pray through Psalm 139: "Search me, God."[xix] Clean up the internal messes before moving onto the external ones. Take time to hear from the board and the executive team about the things that they would like to see changed or repaired before you leave, and then work diligently to clean up projects. Leaving behind a healthy organization is one of the clearest signs of a successful succession. Are there any confessions, apologies, or difficult decisions you need to make for the sake of the mission?

2. **Incoming leader:** While you may have plenty of new ideas and plans, start by listening well to the board, the staff, and the constituents. Consider doing a SWOT analysis in your first ninety days with the staff and board to ensure there is alignment about the state of the organization and its current needs. When I (Doug) arrived at Marketplace Chaplains, I asked staff to consider on the first day: What is complicated and where are we stuck? What needs to be simplified or clarified? Where do you need to

be empowered? Five years later, we continue to ask these same questions, and they continue to provide extraordinary clarity and guidance.

Sometimes, staff and board members may have complaints about the previous leader. If so, set times to listen one on one or in small teams. As much as possible, seek to honor your predecessor and reinforce a focus on the future, not the past. Invite team members to help build the future.

3. **Board:** Before the new leader arrives, pay attention to the tough or delayed decisions. Take action where possible instead of leaving any unnecessary messes for the new leader. Consider completing a SWOT analysis, asking staff and other constituents to identify strengths, weaknesses, opportunities, and threats in the current moment. After cleaning up any unfinished business, lean into the future. Plan a spiritual retreat with the new leader to establish relationships, pray together, and dream for the future.

    Just as leaders should consider whether they are the right person to lead the organization through the next season, ask the same question of the board: Are the current board members

Peter Greer and Doug Fagerstrom

the best to lead in this next season? Have some members become so intertwined with the outgoing leader that they can no longer be objective? Author Ruth Haley Barton wisely wrote, "It is important to involve the right people. ... One very common leadership mistake is to think that we can take a group of undiscerning individuals and expect them to show up in a leadership setting and all of a sudden become discerning."[xx]

4. **Staff:** Before the outgoing leader exits, take time to identify any organizational gaps. What needs to be cleaned up before the new leader steps in? Who is the best person to help accomplish those things? Like any change, transition can provoke grief. And, it's impossible to fully welcome the incoming leader without taking the time to say goodbye to the outgoing leader. Take time for a "good goodbye"—likely with a few laughs and tears—as the outgoing leader leaves and be prepared to celebrate as the new leader steps into the role.[xxi]

158

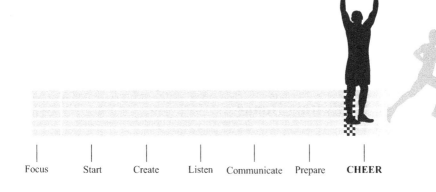

11

CHEER ON THE TEAM

More than any other track-and-field activity, relay racers understand that the race is a team sport. This event requires dependence on teammates to run well and to facilitate a smooth hand off. You only celebrate when all runners finish.

To be a relay runner means to run with the best you've got and then to cheer on your teammate as they accelerate past you. Some runners, after running their leg, quickly lose momentum and collapse. But others, even as they catch their breath, cheer for their teammate to run the next leg with endurance and to steward the baton well.

Cultivating Honor

When Tom Lin stepped into the president position at InterVarsity, he was intentional about honoring and respecting Alec Hill, the former president. Alec had promoted Tom to vice president six years earlier. Their relational trust was deep, and Tom continued this friendship even when he took the baton.

In speaking separately with both of them, we were most impressed by their shared respect for each other. When asked probing questions about what could have been improved or what moments they wished they could redo in the succession process, they owned their own limits but never spoke anything even mildly critical of the other.

This stands out from other transitions, where it is clear that deep hurt and resentment existed between the people who experienced both sides of the transition. Perhaps stemming from insecurity, the outgoing leader may have tried to highlight the failures of the new leader or the new leader might have ensured that stakeholders knew the faults of the predecessor, so that they might not be inadvertently blamed.

But in the healthiest transitions, leaders respect and honor one another.

Tom honored Alec and the InterVarsity team by stepping in with a posture of learning. When he entered the role, Tom developed a list of the top fifty people to talk to in the first ninety days. In his calls, he asked what they saw at InterVarsity. Eager to learn, Tom listened attentively and proactively. Not only that, Tom also initiated quarterly calls with Alec to get on the same page and talk through various questions. He carried a "ministry of presence" around the office, making sure that he was around and available in the first ninety days, especially.

Alec honored Tom by making sure he did not cast a shadow over Tom's leadership. He didn't want to appear like a threat to the work that Tom was doing. With undivided support, he stepped off the stage to the front row seat, where he could cheer loudly and wholeheartedly. His goal was to become the chief cheerleader for Tom as quickly as possible. When staff asked him questions, he didn't speculate or share his opinions. "I don't know. Just go check with Tom," he'd say. Lastly, he kept personal relationships with staff and supporters but officially transferred all the work relationships to Tom.[i]

Honoring others is just not a nice idea; it is a directive from God, who admonishes us to "honor one another above yourselves."[ii]

On a very practical note, Fred Smith, founder of the Gathering, shares, "Never call the next president your successor if you are the founder. ... The word "successor" ties them to you for their identity."[iii] While you're at it, replace the pronoun "I" with "we" whenever possible. It's a subtle reminder of the collective work we are doing together.

Letting Go

After the moment of transition, there should be no ongoing operational mandates left to the outgoing leader. Price Harding understands the danger that comes with a leader who won't let go. He shares that succession doesn't go well when there are continual directives such as "this person needs to be fired," or "you cannot fire my nephew," or "here is your strategic plan—now execute it!" These are all recipes for succession failure.[iv]

He continues, "Incumbent leaders (rightfully) believe that God has called them to steward the organizational mission, so they are reluctant to even begin turning that over to someone else. Oftentimes, they will not fully turn over responsibility until their successor is in place for years. Moreover, they believe that everything (they did) is part of the organization's 'secret sauce' and so, out of good intentions, they will often resist even minor changes brought in by the new leadership, believing that these minor changes will be the undoing of the organization. If the new leader adopts a dress code that no longer requires men to wear ties, the incumbent will often see that as an indication that the future of the organization and its mission have been severely compromised."

Leaders who transition successfully recognize that their successor will not do everything the way they did—and it's OK! They're willing to let go of their preferences while holding tightly to the mission. They give true freedom for the new leader to lead. As St. Augustine has often been quoted to say, "In essentials, unity; in non-essentials, liberty; in all things, charity."[v]

In healthy transitions, exiting leaders become chief cheerleaders of the mission and the new leader.

ACTION STEPS:

Cheer on the Team

1. **Outgoing Leader:** As with any follower of Christ, the fruit of the Spirit should truly radi-

ate, especially during this time. How you lead through this transition will be remembered! Express freedom and flexibility in how the mission will be accomplished in the next season and offer your enthusiastic support of the new leader.

2. **Incoming Leader:** Publicly acknowledge and affirm your predecessor, even if you didn't agree with all of the decisions they made during their tenure. The way a leader honors their predecessor (and others!) will help to establish a culture of honor.

3. **Board:** During this time, the board should be extra attentive to honor both leaders and the staff as a way of easing fears and strengthening the organization. When the new board chair of Marketplace Chaplains asked for time with the staff, she started by disarming fears and concerns and simply sharing her testimony, love for God, and excitement about the mission. Staff left the time feeling encouraged and empowered. Sharing from a place of vulnerability welcomed a culture of humility and harmony.

4. **Staff:** How might the team better live out the "one anothers" of the New Testament? By

loving one another, encouraging one another, building up one another, honoring one another, forgiving one another, serving one another, and more, the team can help to create space and a sense of belonging.

CONCLUSION

In the best relay races, there is calibration.

The runners are in the best positions; their strengths align with the strengths needed for their respective leg of the race. They know that they're not running for themselves but for a team and a common mission. They have already put in the work needed for a successful run and handoff. With a clear plan in place, they heed their coach's wisdom and communicate clearly with one another. Even on a crowded track, teammates line up in the right lane with a focus on each other. They hand off and receive the baton with ease, cheering for each other and celebrating the advancement of the baton in the race.

In many ways, successful successions in our organizations look similar to successful relays on the racetrack—from a steadfast focus on the mission to a clear plan to a celebratory handoff and more. It's a gift to steward the baton for a time, but an even greater joy to pass it off and watch it advance as others take hold.

When considering leaders who have modeled a healthy passing of the baton, we celebrate the transition at East-West Ministries International. From start to finish, the leaders had alignment, understood their race, and successfully passed the baton.

In 2010, founder John Maisel passed the baton to teammate Kurt Nelson, creating a successful succession for the mission of East-West Ministries, an organization focused on reaching the unreached with the light of the Gospel.

Though John and Kurt have very different personalities and leadership styles, the two carry a similar unwavering focus on the East-West mission. As John prepared his heart for transition, he shared, "The cornerstone of East-West is lostness and getting the Gospel to the ears of as many people as possible globally, and Kurt shares that conviction. Even though we differ from one another, our goals and objectives are the same."

From the start, the two leaders focused on the whole race. They embraced the Kingdom mission above personal legacies or accolades. Authentic character and clear direction kept the mission strong. Together, John and Kurt agreed that if the leadership was not right with God, the ministry would not be right. John noted that the founder or outgoing CEO is handing off what God built, not what he or she built. "God owns the ministry, and as founders, our biggest fight is with our own hearts in thinking that we are more important than we really are."

Both John and Kurt prepared their hearts and minds significantly for transition. John credits God for his successes in the transition, noting that the Lord prepared his heart in moments of prayer and Scripture reading before, during, and after the transition took place. He said, "The outgoing leader must have a deep commitment to do everything they can to promote loyalty, confidence, and credibility to the new leader in empowering them to be successful. There has been no talking behind Kurt's back, no lobbying with board members, and no complaining."

It wasn't just that these two leaders focused on the whole mission as they started preparing their hearts and minds for transition. It was that they also created a plan to put succession into action, including the shared commitment to prayer. Kurt and John prayed over the transition and invited the board, staff, and constituents to pray as well. Knowing he couldn't lead on his own, Kurt surrendered to God, allowing the Holy Spirit to lead through him.

After prayer and surrender, Kurt and John put a plan into action, noting that "the further ahead [you plan], the better!" They engaged the board in a timely fashion to discuss and agree on the terms of character, competencies, leadership experience, and education to empower the organization to recruit excellent external candidates or develop qualified internal candidates.

Reflecting on the story of Moses and Joshua, Kurt explained, "As Moses was a submitted servant to the Lord, he soon trained up another servant, Joshua, to take his place. In a similar way, John mentored and coached me for fourteen years in order to prepare me to receive the baton of leadership from him and from the Lord."

And after fourteen years, when it was time for Kurt to step into the CEO role, he and John communicated clearly with each other, with the board, with the staff, and with the constituents. As they prepared for the baton pass, John transferred his personal long-term relationships to Kurt to establish a stronger constituency.

When Kurt officially transitioned, the board hosted a public ceremony with ministry partners and friends to champion Kurt in his new role. At the celebration, John and the board chairman laid hands, prayed, and commissioned Kurt as CEO.

As a way to honor Kurt, John immediately stepped back and created space for Kurt to lead without his shadow. He celebrated the team Kurt built and remained available for anything Kurt needed without overstepping. "It's so important that a founder gives the next person freedom, even to fail. I believe that God is more committed to the process than to success," he shared. The two leaders keep short accounts with each other by meeting off site once a month to address any misgivings in humility and grace.

Since the transition, Kurt has acknowledged that the greatest lesson he learned through the process was humility. He shares, "I've had to walk in deep humility and confidence that God was not asking me to have the same personality as John; rather, I needed to be comfortable in my own skin and let God lead through my unique gifts."[i]

At the end of the day, it mattered more to John and Kurt that they were faithful to God rather than successful in the eyes of others.

Longing for More

We long for more leaders and organizations to navigate this moment like John and Kurt: to prepare faithfully, pray fervently, run well, and finish strong.

Several years ago, Dr. J. Robert Clinton, Fuller Seminary professor, did a study which revealed alarming results. Analyzing leaders throughout the Bible, he found that only one out of three maintained a dynamic relationship with God to the end.[ii]

Only one in three finished well. Only one in

three successfully ran to the end and passed the baton of faith to the next generation. In our experience, we've seen a similar percentage of organizations effectively manage their season of succession.

That's simply not good enough! Our work matters, and we are eager to see organizations manage this season with wisdom, grace, and a commitment to the long-term implementation of their mission.

What would it mean for us to "finish well" in succession planning? What would it look like to rest knowing that we ran with everything we had and to celebrate with joy as the next runner firmly grasped the baton and accelerated beyond us?

At HOPE International, our board manual expresses the brief, extraordinary opportunity that board members have to advance the mission. It reads: "We are relay racers who are handed a 'baton' and given the responsibility to not drop it but run forward faithfully with it. We are responsible for what we do not own. Success is achieved when we leave behind an organization that is stronger and healthier on the day we pass forward the baton than on the day we first took it."[iii]

Organizationally, passing off the baton means passing off the financial, operational, spiritual, and relational aspects of the organization. This a celebration that is not marked by a medal, but by depth of relationships, by excitement about your future and excitement about the organization's future. It means that you're cheering for your team and for the new leader on the sidelines—ready to help but not interjecting in ways that undermine the new leader.

David J. Gyertson writes, "Intentionally orchestrating the CEO transition can be one of the greatest opportunities to re-energize vision … assess current conditions, reengineer structures, strategically reallocate resources, and deploy the right people for God's next season of ministry and service effectiveness."[iv]

Stories Worth Telling

Dan Williams, director of integrated strategy at HOPE International, competed in track and field at the University of South Carolina. He enthusiastically shared with us the essential elements in a relay race that we included in this book. And I (Peter) might be wrong, but as he spoke, I thought I could hear the excitement rising in his voice as he shared certain moments and techniques from his years spent on the track.

When we asked him to tell us his most memorable relay experience, he paused before launching into a story about a 2002 race. It was a race where South Carolina had no shot at winning. Due to a heroic performance from all runners, however, there was a complete upset against several perennial powerhouse teams.

Ironically, Dan wasn't even at the University of South Carolina at that time. He was in tenth grade. Yet, when we asked him about his most memorable story, he shared about a team that came before him. Previous runners inspired Dan and future generations in how well they ran their race.

We want to be leaders who finish our races well—creating missional stories worth telling.

Gratitude

John Coors Sr. built a large manufacturing supply business for aerospace, medical, chemical, and oil and gas companies. After a forty-year career, John retired and passed off his business to his sons. Friends, family, and colleagues gathered at his retirement party in the foothills of the Rocky Mountains just outside of Denver, Colorado, to celebrate him and his legacy. When I (Doug) asked John what he would say to summarize his years of leadership, he kindly and humbly looked at me and said, "I can get that into one word: gratitude."[v]

Someday, we hope to echo John's word.

As you think about succession planning, what

would it look like to leave a legacy of gratitude?

Imagine if we walked out of our organizations with an overwhelming sense of gratitude for our time in the race: for the friends and family who had cheered us on and sacrificed right alongside us, for the colleagues who ran with us and carried us when our legs were weak, for the board who generously offered wisdom and guidance and encouragement.

Imagine if we walked out of our organizations deeply grateful for the advancement of the mission: for the men and women who ran ahead of us to cultivate the organization's identity and purpose; for the leaders of the next generation who will take up the baton to run with endurance and conviction, taking the organization further than we could have on our own.

Imagine if we walked out of our organizations thanking God for His faithfulness: for the understanding that our identity is secure not by the title on our business cards, but by our adoption as God's dearly loved sons and daughters. Imagine if we truly felt freedom to let go, to trust, and to rest in the confidence that His Kingdom will come—yes, even without us.

"All were commended for their faith, but none of them received what had been promised, since God had planned something better for us so that only together with us would they be made perfect. Therefore, since we are surrounded by such a great cloud of witnesses, let us throw off everything that hinders and the sin that so easily entangles. And let us run with perseverance the race marked out for us, fixing our eyes on Jesus, the pioneer and perfecter of faith."

Hebrews 11:39-12:2

ACKNOWLEDGEMENTS

What do running a relay race and writing a book have in common? They're both a team effort! We're abundantly grateful for the many friends who contributed to this book.

To the leaders who graciously shared their stories of succession with us: Leith Anderson, Dan Wolgemuth, Tiger Dawson, Chris Crane, Dana Doll, Jack Crowley, Rick Rutter, Dr. Peter Teague, Jena Lee Nardella, Justin Straight, Mark Linsz, Tom Lin, Alec Hill, Paul Tokunaga, Mike Sharrow, Buck Jacobs, Paul Marty, Sandy Schultz, Bob Gehman, John Maisel, Kurt Nelson, and John Coors Sr. We are incredibly grateful for the way you candidly shared about both successes and failures in leadership transition. Those conversations not only shaped this manuscript, but they helped to strengthen our own succession planning processes.

To the friends who offered keen insights and thoughtful wisdom on succession planning: Phil Clemens, Scott Messner, Paul Park, Fred Smith, Russ Crosson, Kelly Steinweg, Bryan Doo, Brian Lewis, Russ Debenport, David Weekley, Steve Douglass, Charlie Kreider, Alan Barnhart, Terry Looper, Dr. David J. Gyertson, Dr. Andy Bunn, Mario Zandstra,

Bruce Dingman, Price Harding, Greg Barnes, and Chuck Shinn. Thank you for giving us the time and space to learn from you. This book is infinitely better because each of you played a part in it!

To the many editors who read the drafts and made significant improvements: Ashley Dickens, Daniel Rice, Chris Horst, Rachel Spier Weaver, Ray Chung, Emma Lown, and Sarah Beth Spraggins. Your attention to details both large and small has not gone unnoticed. Thank you for your editorial contributions.

To Dan Williams: We learned more about skillful baton passes in one conversation with you than we had in our whole lives. Thanks for sharing your techniques, best practices, and stories with us.

To Dan Busby: Thank you for writing the foreword to this book—just 10 days after stepping down from your role at the ECFA, no less! We're grateful for your example in leading and leaving well.

To the designers: Andrea Fahnestock, Kelly Ryan, and Grace Engard. Thank you for your collaboration and openhandedness to design this book.

To the boards of HOPE International and Marketplace Chaplains: Thank you for giving us the opportunity to lead in this season and helping us to discern our time to transition.

To our families: Thank you for actively and enthusiastically supporting yet another writing project. You are our biggest fans in this and in so many other endeavors!

To our Savior, Jesus Christ: Thank you for showing us how to do succession planning well. Soli Deo Gloria.

APPENDICES

APPENDIX 1:

How prepared are you for your succession?

While there is no tried-and-true way to ensure that your succession will be a success, there are several indicators that will set you on the right path. Complete the brief self-assessment below. On a scale of 1 to 5, record your opinion on the following statements about your succession plan.

    1 = Disagree

    2 = Somewhat Disagree

    3 = Neutral

    4 = Somewhat Agree

    5 = Agree

Once you have completed the assessment, discuss your responses with your board. Where is there alignment or misalignment in your responses? How might you better prepare for your succession?

Postures

The Mission: What matters most?

1. I recognize this mission will extend far beyond this moment I've been entrusted to it.
2. I am focused more on the mission than my own legacy.

The Myths: What lies do I believe?

1. I believe I am not indispensable.
2. I am actively planning and preparing for my succession.
3. We have structures to prioritize conversations around succession planning.
4. I am actively sharing the blessing of leading.

The Moment: Is it time?

1. I am protecting and prioritizing space to listen to God.
2. My skills align with this stage of the organization.
3. I trust that God has others who could lead even better than I can.
4. The board is more committed to the mission than to me as a leader.

The Mirror: Where is my identity?

1. I spend more time and energy considering long-term organizational health than self-preservation.
2. My identity is not defined by my title and role.
3. My actions are marked more by trust than fear in succession planning.
4. My actions are marked more by humility than pride in succession planning.
5. I want people to remember more what God did than what I did.

Practices

Focus on the whole race

1. The mission of the organization is clearly articulated.
2. I believe the mission matters most.
3. I have implemented regular reminders, like a resignation letter, to help me to remember my role as a steward of this mission for a time.

Start training now

1. I am actively investing in future leaders by sharing the platform and giving them the opportunity to grow and develop into leadership roles.

2. The board has clearly defined characteristics of an ideal successor.
3. I have listed the attitudes, obstacles, and fears that might prevent me from fully letting go when it's time to transition.
4. To hurdle the psychological barrier, I've said aloud to myself, "I will transition."
5. The board has a conversation about succession planning on (at least) an annual basis.

Create the plan

1. I am actively planning for and discussing succession with the board.
2. The board has developed an emergency succession plan in the case of a sudden leadership transition.
3. The board has developed a long-term succession plan to put into place the moment I announce my transition.
4. Every year, I give the board a short list of people—internal and external—who could lead in the president or CEO position with excellence.
5. The organization would be able to sustain operations and fundraising activities without me.

Listen to the coach

1. There is a mentor or a coach who is walking with me now as I plan and prepare for my exit, even if it's years away.

Communicate clearly

1. Staff do (or will) have space to grieve.
2. I am confident every stakeholder understands the mission.
3. I've initiated conversations with board members about things that seem confusing or complicated about the mission or vision.
4. The board has discussed gaps in communication and clarity in the succession plan.

Prepare for the handoff

1. I am making tough decisions now, not leaving a mess for my successor to clean up.
2. I am committed to finishing strong, not coasting.
3. I have apologized to the people I have wronged.
4. The board and the executive team have openly shared things that they would like to see changed or fixed before I leave.
5. The organization will not lose institutional knowledge and contacts if I were to suddenly leave.

Cheer on the team

1. I pray regularly for my successor, whoever he or she may be.
2. I have a plan for clarifying boundaries and appropriately stepping away.
3. I am committed to cheering on the new leader.

APPENDIX 2:

Sample survey of staff needs

During a succession process, the board may consider asking for feedback from staff and constituents. Some have found it helpful to release a survey to staff once they've been informed of a plan for succession as early buy-in is important for organizational health. Below, please find a sample survey to kickstart the process of listening to staff regarding succession planning.

Rate the following on a scale of 1 (not important) to 5 (important).

I hope the new leader will provide:

Organizational Leadership Skills:

1 2 3 4 5 Solid structures and systems

1 2 3 4 5 Collaborative style

1 2 3 4 5 Visionary leadership

1 2 3 4 5 Innovative and futuristic thinking

1 2 3 4 5 Equipping and training

1 2 3 4 5 Strong communication

1 2 3 4 5 Experience in our type of mission

1 2 3 4 5 Experience in starting and growing an organization

Personal Leadership Character Traits:

1 2 3 4 5 Culture of care and empathy

1 2 3 4 5 Emotional support

1 2 3 4 5 Spiritual guidance as a shepherd leader

1 2 3 4 5 Encouragement

1 2 3 4 5 Unity

1 2 3 4 5 Positivity and optimism

1 2 3 4 5 Spontaneity

1 2 3 4 5 Discipline

APPENDIX 3:

Which search firms are recommended?

What will an outside search firm offer? Search firms provide objective, professional counsel to the board and mission. With proven tools and instruments, the firm can better assess an organization and its incoming leader. Not only that, but a search firm tends to have a broader reach that stretches beyond the organization's current constituency and limited network.

1. When should we consider a search firm?

There are several different scenarios when an organization might consider a search firm. If there is no obvious successor in the organization, the board might consider reaching out to a search firm to help develop a candidate pool. If there are several potential candidates, a search firm might be a helpful objective voice to give professional and well-vetted recommendations to the search committee or the board. Lastly, if all current attempts to find a successor have not yielded confidence or unanimity among the leadership, a search firm may offer some guidance.

2. How can we find and vet a search firm that best fits our mission?

Perhaps one of the biggest concerns about hiring an outside search firm is finding a firm that doesn't elevate or prioritize the mission in their search. To avoid this, invite other organizations to share their own stories of using an outside firm. Seek out recommendations of those who did it well. Then, consider searching online to find options of those who were a strong organizational or missional fit. Consider even interviewing two or three firms who you believe will best serve your mission. Pray with your leadership team and ask God for guidance before finalizing a decision.

3. How do the board, the search committee, and the search firm work together?

While the board, the search committee, and the search firm have distinct roles, the three entities should be fully engaged in the process. Communicate regularly, even involving representatives from the other entities where appropriate. The search committee should maintain healthy communication with the staff, the board, and the constituents at all times. Honor each other: the search committee must be able to listen and learn from the professional advice and process offered by the firm, and the firm must help to create healthy communication structures between all organizational groups. As always, keep prayer at the forefront. Let God guide the process.

4. Which search firms are recommended?

Agora Search Group: Agora Search Group specializes in recruiting high-level pastors, leaders, and executives for positions in a variety of sectors. From regional start-ups to global manufacturing firms, Agora works with organizations to find the highest level of talent through their client-centered search process. Learn more at agorasearchgroup.com.

CarterBaldwin Executive Search: Rated by Forbes as one of "America's Best Executive Search Firms," CarterBaldwin is one of the forty largest search firms in the United States. The company conducts searches for C-level executives for clients of businesses, cooperatives, universities, and nonprofit organizations around the world. Reach out to the team at carterbaldwin.com.

The Dingman Company: With 30+ years of experience, The Dingman Company provides strategic counsel that identifies and matches exceptional executive leaders who are aligned with their clients' values, culture, and needs. They counsel boards and CEOs on boardsmanship, board recruiting, compensation, transition planning, and more. Learn more at dingman.com.

Faith Search Partners: Dedicated to providing lasting solutions and championing faith-driven leaders, Faith Search Partners exists to empower faith-based organizations with the right leaders at the right time to help drive their unique mission of ministry forward. Every day, they work to fulfill a greater purpose that extends beyond the day-to-day details and ventures into the larger stories of the people and organizations they serve. Find out more information at faithsearch-partners.com.

Macaulay Search: Macaulay Search provides executive search services for organizations with strong social, ethical, or charitable objectives. Reputed for their focused ownership, quality, and efficiency, Macaulay offers a people-focused approach that assists clients in finding several appointable candidates and supports candidates in identifying the right fit for their skills and passions. To learn more, visit macaulaysearch.com.

NL Moore & Associates: NL Moore & Associates support churches in search processes, pastoral successions, congregational assessments, and coaching for a variety of stakeholders. Committed to helping the local church to thrive, the NL Moore & Associates team offers cost-effective, comprehensive, and scalable consulting services. Learn more at nlmoore.com.

North Group Consultants: Through sustained relationships, the team at North Group supports the development of leaders and organizations toward their highest potential. Their work focuses specifically on character development and self-awareness development. North Group offers a wide array of services including executive transition solutions, leadership and organizational development, and health and performance assessments. Learn more at northgroupconsultants.com.

The Shepherd's Staff: The Shepherd's Staff equips churches of all different sizes and denominations to attract, engage, and select new leadership. Their team offers discovery assessments, opportunity profiles, trainings, vettings, and more. To learn more, visit theshepherdsstaff.com.

Slingshot Group: The Slingshot Group offers staffing, coaching, and succession planning services to nonprofits and churches. To share best practices in hiring and transitioning, the Slingshot Group also provides a variety of resources—including videos, eBooks, podcasts, online courses, and events—on their website. Find out more information at slingshotgroup.com.

Vanderbloemen: With over 250 years of combined experience in Christian leadership, Vanderbloemen serves churches, schools, nonprofits, family offices, and values-based businesses. Together with 12+ network strategic partners, Vanderbloemen works with their clients to build strong teams and appoint next-generation leadership. For more information, visit vanderbloemen.com.

APPENDIX 4:

Suggested timeline for a succession plan

The best time to start planning for a succession is now. Below, please find a recommended timeline to implement when actively working toward succession. Of course, every organization looks different, and their succession plans and timelines will look different, too. Our hope is that this is a helpful guide to an outgoing leader and a governing board to oversee and kickstart the planning.

Note: If the outgoing leader makes a sudden exit, the suggested stages will be employed in a much quicker timeframe, and there may even be a need for interim leadership.

Methodical Long-Term Plan (Suggested timeline: 9-12 months):

Stage 1 | Pray and reflect: The outgoing leader prays about his or her own transition and processes it personally before sharing with the board. The heart posture of a transition comes before the practices.

Stage 2 | Invite others in: The outgoing leader shares

thoughts of his or her transition with the board chair and one other board member. This group of three is committed to praying and seeking the heart of God. All questions and concerns should be equally shared among these three confidants. (Don't rush this time. Everyone will need the time to think, pray, and process.) When this trusted group is convinced it is time to move forward with succession, the board is called together and the outgoing leader shares about his or her plans to transition.

Stage 3 | Appoint a search team and alert staff: With prayer, clarity, and confidentiality, the board talks through the decision together and appoints a search team. The search team may be composed of fully informed and engaged missional stakeholders, but it is best to have at least two members from the board on the search team. After this meeting, the outgoing leader plans a meeting with the staff, and the board crafts an announcement to inform stakeholders.

Stage 4 | Build a timeline: The board and search team create a step-by-step plan together for the remaining months. They include all of the organizational areas that need attention before the outgoing leader's transition. For example, all policy manuals, job descriptions, organizational charts, website, collateral materials, current projects, and missional plans should be up to date. Make sure to clarify communication plans for all stakeholders and the outgoing leader's role after the transition. Lastly, this is the time to start the conversation on possibly hiring a search firm; assign certain board or search team members to investigate possibilities. The outgoing leader should maintain a balance of full engagement and delegation.

Stage 5a | Hire a search firm (optional): The board meets to narrow the search firm possibilities down to two firms. They prepare relevant materials that will be helpful to a search firm (and to the incoming leader), including job description, organizational history, strategic plans, annual reports, collateral materials, staff profiles, missional results, challenges, and opportunities. After contacting the two firms, the board and search team review the firm's proposals together and pray. The board meets with the two firms for interviews. After deliberation and prayer, the board decides on one firm together. Guided by the search firm, the board and search team work with one another to find, vet, and recommend candidates. Depending on the mission and job requirements, this stage could take several months.

Stage 5b | Let the search team guide the process: If a firm is not chosen, the search team will need the next several months to guide the process. The search team may consider the following steps:

1. Meet every week and maintain ongoing communication with the board.
2. Create a complete profile of the mission, ministry, and role.
3. Solicit input from key stakeholders regarding essential skills, knowledge, abilities, and attributes of the organization's next leader. Consider who would be an ideal leader for the organization over the next decade.
4. Explore all possible networks in the search of potential candidates.
5. With recommendations from trusted friends of the mission and applications from potential candidates, keep note of every application with a rating process.
6. Narrow the list to the top five to seven qualified candidates and schedule interviews.
7. Interview the candidates with the same predetermined set of questions, then narrow the search to the top two or three candidates. Invite them in for live interviews.

8. Pray and discern together. If needed, add in another interview or two with the top candidate (and even his or her spouse, if necessary).

Stage 6 | Extend an offer: Once the team is in agreement about the best candidate for the position, extend the offer.

Stage 7 | Celebrate: Don't forget to celebrate! Appropriately honor the outgoing leader and welcome the incoming leader through a commissioning celebration.

Short Term Unexpected Plan (6 months):

In the event of a sudden departure, the board must modify some of the process notes listed above. Every situation will be different, but many of the preparation principles still apply. Depending on the circumstances, the board may need to identify and appoint an interim leader.

APPENDIX 5:

Unique successions

Incoming leaders may face a host of joys and challenges, regardless of whom they follow. Here are just a few considerations when following a founder, a family member, a successful leader, or an unsuccessful leader. Whenever possible, find someone who has walked a similar road and learn from them.

Founder: With an entrepreneurial spirit and exceptional tenacity, founders are uniquely gifted. For some, starting an organization may even compare to giving birth and raising a child. For this reason, succession may feel especially like a "loss" for a founder.

As a new leader, be extra sensitive and empathetic in the succession planning process. Be aware of heightened levels of sensitivity and a critical spirit toward change while finding ways to honor, respect, and value the contributions of the founder.

In their article, "Making Founder Successions Work," the authors note, "In the world of corporate startups, four out of five founders are forced out by their boards. And search-firm executives cite how rarely CEO successors call on former bosses. Al-

Peter Greer and Doug Fagerstrom

though some social sector research supports keeping founders involved, clean breaks tend to be the rule."[i] Work with the board to establish and clarify expectations, especially regarding a clean break. As always, give the staff and board time to adjust to this transition.

Family Member: In family transitions, it's important to recognize the propensity for heightened emotions and expectations. Consider seeking an objective outside coach to navigate these transitions, especially in cases where there are strong loyalties to the outgoing leader. As much as possible, create a clean break and give the next leader the freedom to lead.

As Dr. Barry Corey shares, we are called to live with a "firm center and soft edges."[ii] In this case, the outgoing leader and incoming leader should take time to agree on what's most important—the mission. The rest can be flexible!

Successful Leader: We celebrate success stories, but it may be tough to follow one. What might a new leader do after following a well-loved, successful leader? Start by acknowledging the past and the outgoing leader with gratitude. Avoid competing or comparing leadership styles; instead, create a forward-thinking movement that invites staff, the board, and constituents to work for the mission, rather than a person.

Unsuccessful Leader: When following a leader who has not led well, realize that people may come to the table wounded and disappointed. Some simply want to vent or lament, while others will need time to heal, get healthy again, and move forward. Create a culture of honor and respect by listening to people and refusing to speak negatively about the outgoing leader. Instead of jumping into new ideas or making sweeping organizational changes right away, take time to shepherd people well. Listen to them and use language that moves them forward. Work with them to build new hope for tomorrow.

APPENDIX 6:

Annotated bibliography

Books

Effective Succession Planning: The fifth edition of this book examines how to proactively plan for a succession and address future talent needs before an emergency succession is needed. The book includes many core practices like identifying competencies, clarifying mission and values, planning for critical absences, developing and retaining top performers, assessing current needs, and more. A comprehensive guide, *Effective Succession Planning* covers downsizing, international issues, management, and more.

Hero Maker: *Hero Maker* explores five practices evident in Jesus' ministry and outlines the steps to maximize leadership and shift to a model of multiplication in church and business. As authors Dave Ferguson and Warren Bird explain, "God's power and purpose are best revealed when we train and release others who in turn do likewise."

Managing Transitions: Business consultant William Bridges offers his experience and expertise in the

25th anniversary edition of *Managing Transitions*. To make the most of change, Bridges argues, it's important for staff members to have a purpose, a plan, and a part to play. Updated to reflect a globally-connected workplace, this book speaks directly to managers and offers a practical, actionable guide to minimize disruptions and navigate transitions with excellence.

Succession: With decades of experience, Noel Tichy has worked with companies like Ford, Nokia, Caterpillar, Intel, and others on managing succession well. In his book, *Succession*, he shares a framework for creating an effective transition pipeline for companies at any stage: a multi-billion dollar conglomerate, a family business, a small startup, or a nonprofit. Filling the book with numerous case studies, Tichy explores common pitfalls and best practices of succession planning—"position[ing] leadership talent development and succession where they belong: at the top of every leader's agenda."

Success and Succession: Written from the successor's perspective, *Success and Succession* offers key considerations and strategies to ensure success in a transition and in a business. Eric Hehman, Jay Hummel and Tim Kochis provide practical, insightful advice on timeline, teambuilding, and potential roadblocks. With interviews that speak to the specific joys and challenges of transitioning to a new role, this book equips leaders to navigate this period of uncertainty with wisdom, strategy, preparedness, and grace.

Succession Planning That Works: In this step-by-step guide, Michael Timms equips senior leaders and HR professionals to build a strong succession plan. Timms showcases real-world examples and takes a closer look at the factors that led to their success or failure. The book also includes twenty downloadable templates and tools to increase succession planning efficiency and effectiveness.

The Succession Solution: Promoted as a strategic guide to business succession, *The Succession Solution* offers a foundation and toolkit to equip business leaders to manage transitions effectively. The book includes a variety of considerations in this season, including establishing purpose, examining timelines, uncovering opportunities, and more. Author Bradley Franc provides a straightforward, concise framework for building a strong, successful transition plan.

Ways of the Relay-Racers: Written by culture creator and consultant Brian Lewis, this book describes the essential elements of creating vibrant organizational culture. While succession planning is only a small part of the book's content, the imagery of the book delivers lessons that will shape the underlying culture ("chiseling the baton") of the organization.

Evaluation Instruments: Leadership and Personality Inventories

In planning for a succession, many have found it helpful to evaluate the organization, the board, the leadership, or the culture with various leadership and personality inventories. We've listed a few of our favorites below:

SWOT Analysis: Conduct a SWOT analysis with their staff or board to identify the strengths, weaknesses, opportunities, and threats present in an organization before a transition.

TeamSight: The TeamSight tool can be used to discern how to recognize and manage the strengths of the team and board members. Learn more at teamsight.co.

Professional Dynametric Programs (PDP): Consider utilizing this professional leadership analysis tool to evaluate the incoming candidate. Learn more at PDPGlobal.com.

Myers-Briggs: Utilize this personality assessment to learn more about a leader's personality in four dichotomies: introversion and extraversion, sensing and intuition, thinking and feeling, judging and perceiving. Learn more at myersbriggs.org.

DiSC Personality Profile: This personality profile can be used to learn more about an individual's personality and behavior. Learn more at discprofile.com.

Organizations

The following organizations have a host of succession resources (articles, monographs, videos) on their websites.

Christian Leadership Alliance: The Christian Leadership Alliance (CLA) equips leaders for Kingdom impact by offering opportunities to learn through various resources and tools, engage in collaborative networking relationships, accelerate knowledge and competency in the core disciplines, and disciple one another through proven best practices. For more information, visit christianleadershipalliance.org.

Evangelical Council for Financial Accountability (ECFA) Monographs: The Evangelical Council for Financial Accountability (ECFA) equips and assesses ministries for financial integrity. On a mission to enhance trust in Christ-centered churches and ministries, the ECFA offers accreditation and resources to enhance credibility. For more information, visit ecfa. org. For more information regarding their governance toolbox and principles for successful successions, visit ecfa.org/ToolboxSeries.aspx.

National Association of Evangelicals: The National Association of Evangelicals (NAE) seeks to honor God by connecting and representing evangelical Christians for the purpose of strengthening the voice of evangelicals in the United States. Representing over 45,000 local churches from 40 different denominations, NAE serves more than a million constituents. For more information, visit nae.net.

APPENDIX 7:

Audit of current talent and culture

As an incoming leader steps into a new role, consider sharing information on staff and missional culture.

Talent:

1. Provide a complete organizational chart with the names and roles of each staff member.
2. Provide written job descriptions for each person who reports directly to the incoming leader.
3. Draft a list of staffing gaps for future hires.
4. Create a list of current staff prayer requests.

Culture:

5. Prepare a one-page overview of the history and mission of the organization.
6. Provide the budget with a one-page financial overview of the last five years.
7. Share how the staff and ministry celebrate people and missional wins.
8. Draft an annotated list of key missional victories and benchmarks from the last five years.
9. Create a list of the most significant organizational key performance indicators (KPIs).

APPENDIX 8:

Five mistakes a board should avoid

Provided by Price Harding, CarterBaldwin Executive Search, as printed in the National Association of Evangelicals Magazine, Winter Edition, 2019/20

1. **Delegating succession planning to the CEO:** Selecting the right leader is the most important responsibility of the board, and it should never be delegated to the incumbent leader. As competent as any leader may be, organizations benefit from new thought. The CEO's choice does not give the board its needed influence over the future of the organization.

2. **Committing the role to an internal person:** While an internal person may ultimately be the best selection, the board should not be restricted to a choice of one, as circumstances and board members change. It is unfair to use assured succession as a tool to retain a leader who may later be surprised by major changes.

3. **Hiring in reaction to the incumbent:** Most search committees really struggle to think of their new hire in entirely independent terms— wanting to either replicate or avoid at all costs the characteristics of the incumbent CEO. The board or search committee needs to think only about the organization—its mission and its future—and to find the leader who can most likely bring its future and mission to fruition.

4. **Allowing the philosophical to conflict with the practical:** The perfect theoretical candidate will always be stronger than the real people God uses to lead organizations. Moreover, do not expect a highly qualified external candidate to know the peculiarities of your organization as well as a possibly less qualified internal candidate.

5. **Permitting the incumbent to determine his or her future role:** The board needs to define what role, if any, the incumbent leader will have in the administration of the new leader. While emeritus titles are honoring, the new CEO should not be hamstrung by a board's sentimental or even practical commitments to the incumbent. There is no greater gift to give to a departing leader than to cap his or her tenure with the assurance

of the organization's continued success. And a departing leader's legacy can only flourish if the succeeding candidate actually succeeds and that must become the sole point of focus for a responsible board in any succession consideration.

ABOUT THE AUTHORS

Peter Greer

Peter Greer is president and CEO of HOPE International, a global Christ-centered microenterprise development organization serving throughout Africa, Asia, Latin America, and Eastern Europe. Prior to joining HOPE, Peter worked internationally as a microfinance adviser in Cambodia and Zimbabwe and as managing director of Urwego Bank in Rwanda. He is a graduate of Messiah University and received a master's in public policy from Harvard's Kennedy School. Peter has coauthored over 10 books, including *Mission Drift* and *Rooting for Rivals*. More important than his occupation is his role as husband to Laurel and dad to Keith, Liliana, Myles, and London. For more information, visit peterkgreer.com.

Doug Fagerstrom

Dr. Doug Fagerstrom is president and CEO of Marketplace Chaplains. Doug came to Marketplace with nearly 31 years of pastoral ministry experience. He served as senior vice president of Converge Worldwide and president of Grand Rapids Theological Seminary. Doug has authored or co-authored fourteen books in Christian ministry and leadership, while also completing a terminal degree with a focus on mentorship of the laity in the local church. Doug brings a theological acumen to the ministry, as well as leadership experience in national and international organizations. Doug and Donna began their journey together as high school students serving through a local Youth for Christ ministry. They are blessed with their daughter and son-in-law who serve as professionals and ministry volunteers. They have two granddaughters who bring them deep joy. Personal pursuits for Doug and Donna include family, travel, writing, equipping others, and growing in ministry.

Brianna Lapp

Brianna Lapp is the executive writing assistant at HOPE International, where she works on a variety of writing projects to advance the mission of HOPE. Brianna graduated from Messiah University with an English degree. She and her husband, Nate, live in Lancaster, Pennsylvania.

ABOUT THE ORGANIZATIONS

HOPE International

HOPE International invests in the dreams of families in the world's underserved communities as we proclaim and live the Gospel. HOPE provides discipleship, biblically based training, savings services, and loans that empower women and men to provide for their families and strengthen their communities. For specific resources on HOPE's approach to spiritual integration, operations, fundraising, governance, and more, visit hopeinternational.org/resources.

Marketplace Chaplains

Marketplace Chaplains is the largest and longest continuing provider of workplace chaplains to corporate America today and exists to share the love of God to employees in the workplace by providing an employee care service through chaplain teams. Over 1,700 chaplains now serve in all 50 states and Canada, providing personal care for more than one million employees and family members. For more information about Marketplace Chaplains, visit mchapusa.com.

RELATED WORKS

Mission Drift

Mission Drift equips leaders to keep their organizations "Mission True" or get back on track. Supported by research and filled with anecdotes, Chris Horst and Peter Greer identify organizations that exhibit intentional, long-term commitments to Christ in contrast to those that have wandered away from their core beliefs.

The Board and the CEO

Good relationships lie at the heart of every successful organization. Yet no relationship is more important—or more challenging—to navigate than the one between the board and the CEO. In this practical and concise book, David Weekley and Peter Greer draw from their years of experience to equip other board members and organizational leaders to enter into an impactful, life-giving partnership.

The Giver and the Gift

The Giver and the Gift outlines a Kingdom perspective on fundraising. David Weekley and Peter Greer help to dismantle certain shaky beliefs and practices, energizing a new generation for generosity and rediscovering a path that values the giver as much as the gift.

NOTES

Foreword

[i] David L. McKenna, *Stewards of a Sacred Trust:* ECFA Press, 2010.

Introduction

[i] Pat Forde, "One message to take from baton blunders: U.S. track has hit rock bottom," *ESPN*, August 21, 2008, espn.com/olympics/summer08/columns/story?columnist=forde_pat&id=3546603

[ii] Ibid.

[iii] "Without a Succession Plan, The Mission of Your Organization is in Jeopardy," *Business Volunteers Unlimited*, February 22, 2018, bvuvolunteers.org/without-a-succession-plan-the-mission-of-your-organization-is-in-jeopardy/

[iv] Jack Crowley, interview with Peter Greer, January 31, 2020.

[v] Fred Smith, email correspondence with Peter Greer, January 27, 2020.

[vi] Greg Barnes, email communication with Doug Fagerstrom.

[vii] Name changed.

[viii] Phil Clemens, interview with Peter Greer, April 6, 2020.

[ix] John 14:12

Chapter 1: The Mission: What matters most?

[i] Drake Baer and Ivan De Luce, "How 18 of the oldest companies on Earth have been making money for centuries, from guns to beer to shipping," *Business Insider*, July 23, 2019, businessinsider.com/oldest-companies-on-earth-2014-8.

[ii] For further reading on the importance of an organization's mission, consider reading *Mission Drift: The Unspoken Crisis Facing Leaders, Charities, and Churches* by Peter Greer and Chris Horst. missiondrift.com/

[iii] "Billy Graham Trivia: What Is Life's Greatest Surprise?" *Billy Graham Evangelistic Association*, March 27, 2017, billygraham.org/story/billy-graham-trivia-lifes-greatest-surprise/.

[iv] Adapted from *40/40 Vision* by Peter Greer and Greg Lafferty

[v] Peter Greer and Greg Lafferty, *40/40 Vision: Clarifying your Mission in Midlife* (Downers Grove, IL: InterVarsity Press, 2015), 155.

[vi] Hebrews 11:39-40

[vii] Colossians 3:23-24

[viii] Justin Straight, interview with Peter Greer, January 15, 2020. There are instances

where missions and organizations are created for shorter-term, time-bound impact.

[ix]Matthew 6:19

Chapter 2: The Myths: What lies do I believe?

[i] Jena Lee Nardella, interview with Peter Greer, January 17, 2020.

[ii] Sadly, this isn't unusual for faith-based boards. In fact, David J. Gyertson notes that there is a "significant tendency" of faith-based boards not to hold CEOs accountable for five primary reasons. First, he writes, boards might have a reluctance to "touch God's anointed"—and instead offer their full trust rather than close scrutiny. Second, boards may overlook certain things, knowing the challenge of finding a new leader (especially if there's a limited salary available). Third, some boards consist of close friends and confidants of the CEO, with their loyalties preventing strong governance. Fourth, board members tend to be too busy with other commitments to devote time to scrutiny. And fifth, CEOs have discouraged thorough oversight, increasing the difficulty of boards to govern well.

[iii] Kim Jonker and William F. Meehan III, "Nothing Succeeds Like Succession," *Stanford Social Innovation Review*, March 12, 2014. ssir.org/articles/entry/nothing_succeeds_like_succession

[iv] If you've been part of a failed baton pass in the past, know that there is hope. Like Jena, consider using your experience to help others; your past mistakes might help to prevent you or others from repeating them. We all fall, and we are all invited to get up and try again. In moments of failure, especially, we are called to be people of grace—as we, too, have been shown grace.

[v] Marty Ozinga III, interview with Brad Formsma, The Wow Factor, podcast audio, January 8, 2020, thewowfactor.libsyn.com/faith-as-a-foundation-ft-marty-ozinga-iii.

[vi] Jonathan Coors, interview with Doug Fagerstrom, January 31, 2020.

[vii] Names changed.

[viii] Mark Linsz, interview with Peter Greer, April 1, 2020.

[ix] Mario Zandstra, email communication with Doug Fagerstrom, May 3, 2020.

[x] Name changed.

[xi] Mario Zandstra, email communication.

Chapter 3: The Moment: Is it time?

[i] Lily Rothman, "Robert Mugabe Ruled Zimbabwe for Decades. Here's How He First Came to Power," *Time Magazine*, September 6, 2019, time.com/4478358/robert-mugabe-dies-history/.

[ii] Ibid.

iii Ibid.

iv Dr. Peter Teague, interview with Peter Greer, January 29, 2020.

v Nathan Sheets, interview with Henry Kaestner, Faith Driven Entrepreneur, podcast audio, September 10, 2019, faithdrivenentrepreneur.org/blog/podcast-episode-73-nathan-sheets-nature-nates-image-management

vi Alec Hill, Living in Bonus Time (Downers Grove, IL: InverVarsity Press, 2020), 137.

vii Rick Rutter, interview with Peter Greer, March 13, 2020.

viii Jack Crowley, interview with Peter Greer, January 31, 2020.

ix Bob Gehman, email communication with Peter Greer, May 6, 2020.

x Tim Alberta, "Americans are Being Held Hostage and Terrorized by the Fringes," POLITICO Magazine, May 13, 2018, politico.com/magazine/story/2018/05/13/arthur-brooks-american-enterprise-institute-interview-218364.

xi Leith Anderson, email communication with Doug Fagerstrom, May 7, 2020.

xii For further reading on seasons, consider Richard Blackaby's Seasons of God. amazon.com/Seasons-God-Shifting-Patterns-Purposes-ebook/dp/B0080Z5HCS/ref=s-r_1_2?dchild=1&keywords=seasons+of+god&qid=1590168271&sr=8-2

xiii Terry Looper, Sacred Pace: Four Steps to Hearing God and Aligning Yourself with His Will (Nashville, TN: W Publishing, 2019), 43.

xiv Dr. Andy Bunn, email communication with Doug Fagerstrom, May 13, 2020.

Chapter 4: The Mirror: Where is my identity?

i Adapted from 40/40 Vision by Peter Greer and Greg Lafferty

ii Ed Dobson, interview with Doug Fagerstrom.

iii Luke 12:22-26

iv Mike Sharrow, interview with Peter Greer, February 17, 2020.

v Ibid.

vi Justin Straight, email communication with Peter Greer, April 27, 2020.

vii Sandy Schutz, interview with Peter Greer, April 16, 2020.

viii John C. Maxwell, The 21 Irrefutable Laws of Leadership (Nashville, TN: Thomas Nelson, 2007), 261.

ix Price Harding, email communication with Doug Fagerstrom, March 24, 2020.

x Patrick Finley, "Bears kicker, Cody Parkey: 'I let fans, teammates, and the whole organization down," Chicago Sun Times, January 11, 2019, chicago.suntimes.

com/2019/1/11/18403109/bears-kicker-cody-parkey-i-let-fans-teammates-and-whole-organization-down.

xi Sharrow, interview.

xii Paul Marty, interview with Peter Greer, February 19, 2020.

Chapter 5: Focus on the Whole Race

i Brian Lewis, *Ways of the Relay Racers: Essays on Leaders, Misleaders, and the Culture-Strong Organization* (Bainbridge Island, WA: Grey Rider West, 2018), 50.

ii Name changed.

iii Russ Crosson, interview with Peter Greer, February 26, 2020.

iv Paul Park, interview with Peter Greer, January 11, 2020.

v Matthew 6:10

Chapter 6: Start Training Now

i Alec Hill, interview with Peter Greer, February 17, 2020.

ii Paul Gompers and Silpa Kovvali, "The Other Diversity Dividend," *Harvard Business Review*, July-August 2018, hbr.org/2018/07/the-other-diversity-dividend#:~:text=The%20Findings,for%20reaping%20its%20business%20benefits.

iii Sharrow, interview.

iv Tiger Dawson, interview with Peter Greer, February 20, 2020.

v Crosson, interview.

vi Marty, interview.

vii Noel Tichy, *Succession: Mastering the Make-or-Break Process of Leadership Transition* (Portfolio, 2014).

viii David J. Gyertson and Bruce Dingman, "Succession Planning For Success," *The Dingman Company*, dingman.com/succession-planning-for-success/.

ix Chad Carter, *Five Attributes: Essentials of Hiring for Christian Organizations* (Mercer Island, WA: Best Christian Workplace Institute, 2016).

x "Leadership that Works: A Study of Theological School Presidents," *Auburn Studies*, December 2010, auburnseminary.org/wp-content/uploads/2016/04/Leadership-That-Works.pdf.

xi Carter, *Five Attributes*, 53.

xii Buck Jacobs, interview with Peter Greer, January 29, 2020.

xiii Kazim Ladimeji, "4 Tips for Selecting a Potent CEO," *Recruiter*, October 30, 2014, recruiter.com/i/4-tips-for-selecting-a-potent-ceo/

[xiv] Warren Bird, "Seven Recent Trends in Leadership Succession," *National Association of Evangelicals*, nae.net/seven-recent-trends-in-leadership-succession/.

[xv] Lewis, *Relay-Racers*, 36-37.

[xvi] Peter Greer and David Weekley, The Board and the CEO (Scotts Valley, CA: Createspace, 2017), 80.

[xvii] Dana Doll, interview with Peter Greer, April 27, 2020.

[xviii] "History of the Navigators," *Navigators*, navigators.org/about/history/

[xix] Genesis 21:33

[xx] Marty Solomon and Brent Billings, The BEMA Podcast, podcast audio, podcasts.apple.com/us/podcast/28-images-of-the-desert-arar-and-tamarisk/id1148115183?i=1000384588684

[xxi] 1 Chronicles 28:2, 6

[xxii] John Caulfield, "Make Your Exit: Succession Planning for a Smooth Leadership Transfer," *Probuilder*, April 2, 2020, probuilder.com/exit-strategy-how-to-create-plan-for-succession.

Chapter 7: Create the Plan

[i] "The Mother of all Relays," *Hood to Coast*, hoodtocoast.com/htc/relay-info/.

[ii] Recently, the board asked Dan to stay for 12 more months as they respond to COVID-19. The plan is still the same, though delayed temporarily.

[iii] Craig Christopher, "Domestiques: The Unsung Heroes of The Tour De France," *Bleacher Report*, July 10, 2010, bleacherreport.com/articles/418356-domestiques-the-unsung-heroes-of-the-tour-de-france

[iv] Dan Wolgemuth, "Youth for Christ Presidential Update," January 21, 2020.

[v] Clemens, interview.

[vi] Ibid.

[vii] Bruce Dingman, email communication with Doug Fagerstrom, March 24, 2020.

[viii] Greg Barnes, email communication with Doug Fagerstrom, May 13, 2020.

Chapter 8: Listen to the Coach

[i] Chris Grenham, "Former Celtics strength coach Bryan Doo continues to connect with players, young and old," *Celtics blog*, January 28, 2019, celticsblog.com/2019/1/28/18196232/celtics-bryan-doo-connect-young-old-boston-harvard-strength-marcus-smart-rozier-brown-jaylen-nba.

[ii] David Norman, interview with Peter Greer, May 22, 2020.

Chapter 9: Communicate Clearly

[i] Gyertson and Dingman, "Successful Planning," *The Dingman Company*, dingman.com/succession-planning-for-success/.

[ii] Chris Crane and Tiger Dawson, email communication with Peter Greer, April 20, 2020.

[iii] Chris Horst, email communication with Peter Greer, April 16, 2020.

[iv] R.T. Watson, Joe Flint, Ben Fritz, "Disney CEO Bob Iger Steps Aside; Bob Chapek Named New Head," *Wall Street Journal*, February 25, 2020, wsj.com/articles/disney-names-new-ceo-to-succeed-iger-11582665764

[v] Brooks Barnes, "Thomas Staggs, Disney's Heir Apparent, Is Stepping Down," *New York Times*, April 5, 2016, nytimes.com/2016/04/05/business/media/thomas-staggs-walt-disney-company.html.

[vi] Russ Debenport, "Leading Change," presentation to HOPE International's executive team, February 12, 2020.

[vii] Russ Debenport, "Change Management in Challenging Times," presentation to HOPE International's global team, June 5, 2020.

[viii] Bradley Franc, *The Succession Solution: The Strategic Guide to Business Transition* (Woodview Publishing, 2019), 44.

[ix] Scott Messner, interview with Peter Greer, March 11, 2020.

Chapter 10: Prepare for the Handoff

[i] "Worst baton pass ever? China's catastrophic 4x100 relay handoff," NBC Sports, published October 6, 2019, youtube.com/watch?v=AV8GNQTOyBU.

[ii] Jason Duaine Hahn, "Chinese Relay Runners Disqualified After Re-Doing Baton Pass Multiple Times During Race, *People Magazine*, October 8, 2019, people.com/sports/chinese-relay-team-baton-pass-fail/.

[iii] Clemens, interview.

[iv] Susan Hogan, "Airbnb Host's Maryland House Trashed to the Tune of $10,000," *NBC Washington*, October 8, 2019, nbcwashington.com/news/local/airbnb-hosts-maryland-house-trashed-to-the-tune-of-10000/1960267/.

[v] "The lifecycle of a CEO," *McKinsey*, assets-prod.mckinsey.com/business-functions/strategy-and-corporate-finance/our-insights/five-fifty-the-lifecycle-of-a-ceo

[vi] Names changed.

[vii] Sharrow, interview.

[viii] Strengths, Weaknesses, Opportunities, Threats (SWOT)

[ix] Names changed.

[x] Mario Zandstra, email communication with Doug Fagerstrom, May 3, 2020.

[xi] Ed Dobson, interview with Doug Fagerstrom.

[xii] Warren Bird, "Seven Recent Trends in Leadership Succession," *National Association of Evangelicals*, nae.net/seven-recent-trends-in-leadership-succession/.

[xiii] Christian Caspar and Michael Halbye, "Making the most of the CEO's last 100 days," *McKinsey*, January 1, 2011, mckinsey.com/featured-insights/leadership/making-the-most-of-the-ceos-last-100-days

[xiv] Schultz, interview.

[xv] "The lifecycle of a CEO," *McKinsey*, assets-prod.mckinsey.com/business-functions/strategy-and-corporate-finance/our-insights/five-fifty-the-lifecycle-of-a-ceo.

[xvi] Eben Harrell, "Succession Planning: What the Research Says," December 2016, hbr.org/2016/12/succession-planning-what-the-research-says

[xvii] Ian Davis, "Letter to a newly appointed CEO," *McKinsey*, June 1, 2010, mckinsey.com/featured-insights/leadership/letter-to-a-newly-appointed-ceo

[xviii] Linsz, interview.

[xix] Psalm 139:23

[xx] Ruth Haley Barton, *Strengthening the Soul of Your Leadership: Seeking God in the Crucible of Ministry* (Downers Grove, IL: InterVarsity Press, 2008), 198.

[xxi] Keith Greer, conversation with Peter Greer, June 10, 2020.

Chapter 11: Cheer on the Team

[i] Tom Lin, interview with Peter Greer, March 12, 2020.

[ii] Romans 12:10

[iii] Fred Smith, email communication with Peter Greer, January 27, 2020.

[iv] Price Harding, email communication with Doug Fagerstrom, March 24, 2020.

[v] Mark Ross, "In Essentials Unity, In Non-Essentials Liberty, In All Things Charity," *Ligonier*, ligonier.org/learn/articles/essentials-unity-non-essentials-liberty-all-things/

Conclusion

[i] John Maisel and Kurt Nelson, email communication with Doug Fagerstrom, April 17, 2020.

[ii] J. Robert Clinton, "Three Articles About Finishing Well," 1999, garyrohrmayer.typepad.com/files/3finishwellarticles.pdf.

[iii] "Board of Directors Manual," *HOPE International*, hopeinternational.org/resources/item/category/governance

[iv] Gyertson and Dingman, "Succession Planning," *The Dingman Company*, dingman.

com/succession-planning-for-success/.

[v] John Coors, interview with Doug Fagerstrom, January 31, 2020.

[i] Jari Toumala, Donald Yeh, Katie Smith Milway, "Making Founder Successions Work," *Stanford Social Innovation Review*, Spring 2018, ssir.org/articles/entry/making_founder_successions_work.

[ii] Dr. Barry Corey, "Love Kindness: Firm Center, Soft Edges," *The Table*, May 11, 2016, cct.biola.edu/love-kindness-firm-center-soft-edges/.

Made in the USA
Middletown, DE
28 August 2020